CANADIAN MARKETING CASEBOOK

FIRST EDITION

CANADIAN MARKETING CASEBOOK

FIRST EDITION

PEGGY CUNNINGHAM
QUEEN'S UNIVERSITY

PRENTICE HALL CANADA INC.
SCARBOROUGH, ONTARIO

© 1999 Prentice-Hall Canada Inc., Scarborough, Ontario
A Division of Simon & Schuster/A Viacom Company

Prentice-Hall, Inc., Upper Saddle River, New Jersey
Prentice-Hall International (UK) Limited, London
Prentice-Hall of Australia, Pty. Limited, Sydney
Prentice-Hall Hispanoamericana, S.A., Mexico City
Prentice-Hall of India Private Limited, New Delhi
Prentice-Hall of Japan, Inc., Tokyo
Simon & Schuster Southeast Asia Private Limited, Singapore
Editora Prentice-Hall do Brasil, Ltda., Rio de Janeiro

ISBN 0-13-973652-2

Publisher: Patrick Ferrier
Acquisitions Editor: Mike Ryan
Production Editor: Kelly Dickson
Copy Editor: Reni Walker
Associate Editor: Sherry Torchinsky
Production Coordinator: Jane Schell
Cover Design: Dave McKay
Page Layout: Steve Eby

1 2 3 4 5   03 02 01 00 99

Printed and bound in Canada.

Visit the Prentice Hall Canada Web site! Send us your comments, browse our
catalogues, and more at **www.phcanada.com**. Or reach us through e-mail at
phcinfo_pubcanada@prenhall.com.

Every reasonable effort has been made to obtain permissions for all articles
and data used in this edition. If errors or omissions have occurred, they will
be corrected in future editions provided written notification has been received
by the publisher.

A CIP catalogue record for this book is available from the National Library
of Canada.

Topical Table of Contents

Preface

This case book has been developed to accompany Prentice Hall Canada marketing texts. Cases are an effective learning tool because they allow students to "experience" marketing as it is practised everyday, rather than learning about marketing by memorizing concepts and terms. Cases encourage students to take a decision-based approach to the marketing discipline.

The cases were selected so that students could have further practice applying the concepts they have studied in various marketing courses. All of the cases are integrative in nature. They require students to synthesize their learning from a number of topic areas. Despite their diversity, the cases all focus on one central theme — the importance of building relationships with customers based upon an understanding buyer behaviour, and customer needs and wants. It is only with this understanding that firms can develop relationship marketing strategies that deliver superior customer value.

The cases were selected because they also reflect the major themes around which most marketing texts are structured: relationship marketing, understanding marketing from a strategic perspective, global marketing, marketing ethics, and marketing in an era technology and rapidly changing environments.

AMPHITRION: YOUR ULTIMATE HOST IN GREECE

Alkis S. Magdalinos[1]

Around the end of October 1993 Constantinos Mitsiou, owner and manager of the Greek Amphitrion Group of Companies, was wondering if he should launch a special tour for teenagers. What he had in mind was a tour lasting fourteen days that would incorporate most of the natural beauty spots of Greece, as well as numerous historic and archaeological sites. He had already concluded a tentative agreement with a couple of professors who would act as guides and worked out a preliminary itinerary, but he was now not sure if he should continue with the idea.

Amphitrion, which started as a travel agency in 1957, was now a large travel and shipping business—'your ultimate hosts in Greece'. The head office of Amphitrion is in Constitution Square, a prestigious business area in the centre of Athens. It also has branches in Tokyo, Washington, DC, and Toronto as well as other Greek offices in Athens, Crete and Piraeus. The largest part of the touring business was for executives and employees of businesses who bought their tickets from the agency branch of the business. These clients also bought family holidays and travel. In 1993, the biggest part of the clientele was middle and senior executives and, sometimes, their secretaries and assistants. Only some 10 per cent of sales come from 'drop-ins', people who casually dropped in at one of Amphitrion's travel offices.

Mr. Mitsiou had first started thinking about his teenager tour after a meeting with other agents at an International Convention, in Milan, in September 1993. He had had a discussion with a travel agent from Rome who told him about a similar exercise he had organized successfully during the last holiday season. He was already thinking of repeating the tour in

---

1. University of LaVerne, Greece

Greece. He also told Mr. Mitsiou that both parents and teenagers looked forward to such tours since it allowed them to have separate vacations. The best time for the tours was between July and August when schools were on holiday. Parents accepted the idea of the tour if the agent could guarantee the proper supervision and the calibre of the people acting as guides.

When Mr. Mitsiou came back to Athens he repeated the idea to Joan and George Lykidis, friends of his, and asked them whether they wanted to act a guides for the tour. Mr. Lykidis was the head teacher of one of Athens' largest schools and a professor of history. Both Mr. and Mrs. Lykidis were enthusiastic about the idea and were eager to take it on.

Mr. Mitsiou did not know if anyone else in Greece had started such a tour. However, he knew that for some years a professor at a well-known school had organized tours of Europe for students from private schools. The activity had developed into a profitable summer business. As far as Mr. Mitsiou knew, the tours were always successful and sold out each year. The teacher used no special advertising for his tours, getting most of his business from old students who had been on the tour themselves and now sent their children.

The tours Mr. Mitsiou had in mind would focus on Greece, including its local colour as well as the important historic and archaeological sites around the country. Characteristically, Mr. Mitsiou said the nature of the tour had occurred to him after reading letters from parents and professors in the daily press. These complained about the theoretical way Greek history was taught at school. To Mr. Mitsiou, it was obvious from the letters that parents and students wanted a tour visiting the sites they had studied so dryly in the history classes. Parents definitely looked forward to giving their children a well-organized tour in which they would visit all these places and where, with proper guidance, the entire history of the ancestry would be revealed to them.

Mr. Mitsiou also knew very well that teenagers would not like it if the whole of the itinerary comprised only visits to museums, and to historic and archaeological sites. He would therefore give them a chance to enjoy the beautiful seashores and beaches; to go into towns and villages; and to have fun at tavernas and discos and enjoy some dancing and entertainment.

After some considerable thought he developed the following itinerary:

Day 1   Departure from Athens—Thermopylae—Tempi—Mount Olympus—Thessaloniki overnight.

Day 2   Morning free. Afternoon visit Eptapyrgio, Old City, St. Demetrious Church, International Fairgrounds, night at a disco, stay overnight at Eptapyrgio.

Day 3   Depart for Philippi, visit sites of interest at Kavala, stay overnight on Thasos Island.

Day 4   Swimming at Golden Beach—Makrynammos, visit Necropolis Museum, return to Kavala, stay overnight.

Day 5   Depart for Polygyros, Agion Oros, swimming at Chalkidiki Beach, overnight in Thessaloniki, go to a disco.

Day 6   Leave for ancient Pella, Vergina, Tomb of Philippos, Grevena, Metosovo, stay overnight.

Day 7   Ioannina, visit Vella Monastery, Ali Pasha Island in Ioannina lake, old town, stay overnight.

Day 8   Dodoni, Arta, Agrinio, Messolonghi, visit sites, Aetolikon, the lagoon, fishing ponds at Tholi, overnight in Messolonghi.

Day 9   Depart for Patras, visit sites, leave for Kyllini, swimming, stay overnight.

Day 10 Leave for Olympia, visit archaeological grounds, overnight in Vityna.

Day 11 Leave for Tripolis, Sparta, visit the museum Mystras, Gythio, Diros caves, Gerolimena for swimming, overnight in Areopolis.

Day 12 Departure for Kalamata, Pylos, Methoni, swimming, return to Malamata, afternoon free, disco, stay overnight.

Day 13 Leave to Tripolis, Nafplio, Tolo, swimming, Tyrins, Argos, Mycenae, Nemea, overnight in Korinth.

Day 14 Ancient Korinth, Sykion, Kiato, Nerantza for swimming, return to Athens.

Mr. Mitsiou knew that tours of this type could be cancelled at the last moment, which would mean that money would have to be refunded. If that happened, the total spending on the promotion of the tour would amount to a loss of about Dr 266,000.[2] In addition, money had to be paid two months in advance to secure good rooms, especially at places with only one hotel, and this would be a significant sum that would have to be written off if the tour did not go ahead. By Mr. Mitsiou's calculation advertising and other expenses would bring the loss to about Dr 1,000,000 if the whole tour was cancelled.

With a group of forty participants on tour, his total cost came to Dr 2,260,000. From this he expected to clear 7 per cent profit. If he had more people on the tour the profits would be greater but George Lykidis had already said that more than forty teenagers would be impossible to supervise properly.

It was important not to cancel the tour in the first year once it had been advertised. Word of mouth was the best way of attracting tour members, particularly as a result of previous members telling their friends. So he decided he would go ahead with as few as twenty participants, but he did not think that he could charge more than Dr 60,450 per person in the first year. When he had organized tours in the past he had used subagents who required a 5 per cent commission. In this project, however, his margins were so small that he would not use subagents.

Soon after he had finished working out the plans for the tour, Mr. Mitsiou met a friend, a very renowned lawyer, who had two sons in their teens. The lawyer said that he would never let his sons go on such a tour. He added that such tours treated teenagers like sheep. Anyhow teenagers had no interest in history, no matter what newspapers said to the contrary. His idea was to give his boys some money and a couple of tickets, and to allow them to travel for as long as the money lasted. For that age group, guides were not important, and it was best to give such teenagers the chance to prove that they were responsible and could travel on their own. This worried Mr. Mitsiou since he always trusted this friend's opinions. He started to reconsider his planned tour and to think of other ways to make the tour look more attractive.

Questions

1. Has Mr. Mitsiou taken a marketing-oriented approach to developing his teenage tour idea? What elements of marketing orientation, if any, are missing?

2. Is the teenage tour idea financially attractive? Does it fit the strengths of the Amphitrion Group? Is it a market that the company naturally understands?

3. Would the tour have been attractive to you as a teenager? Would this Greek tour be attractive to teenagers in your country? Would you have found a similar tour of your own country attractive? Would your parents find it attractive? Who is the customer in this case and what do they want?

4. Is running a tour the only way to see if it would be successful or not? How else do you think its appeal could be tested? How could the tour be changed to be more appealing and less risky?

PROCTER & GAMBLE: FACELLE DIVISION FACIAL TISSUE

IVEY

Professor Terry H. Deutscher prepared this case solely to provide material for class discussion. The author does not intend to illustrate either effective or ineffective handling of a managerial situation. The author may have disguised certain names and other identifying information to protect confidentiality.

Early in March 1992, Randall Beard was reviewing performance of the brands of facial tissue that Procter & Gamble had acquired in August 1991. "Now that we have had a few months to understand the tissue business in Canada," he thought, "it's time to build our plan for the future of the business. P&G hasn't spent $185 million in acquiring the Facelle division in order to stand still in the marketplace."

Although Procter & Gamble had global brands in some categories of paper products (e.g., Pampers, the leading disposable diaper), the Facelle acquisition was P&G's first step outside the U.S. in the tissue/towel business. For that reason, senior management would be closely watching the progress of the Facelle brands of facial tissue, paper towels, and bathroom tissue. In particular, the facial tissue market was especially challenging, as 1991 had seen more competitive product initiatives than the previous several years put together.

As associate advertising manager for Tissue, Towel and Facial Products, Randall Beard reported directly to Barbara Fraser, vice president and general manager of the Paper Products business in Canada. Together, the two would be responsible for several major decisions about the facial tissue brands, including positioning, product formulations, and promotion. For his forthcoming meeting with Fraser, Beard wanted to have a set of definite recommendations on the future of the brands.

THE PROCTER & GAMBLE COMPANY

Procter & Gamble originated in 1837, when William Procter and James Gamble, two immigrant soap and candle makers, formed a partnership in Cincinnati, Ohio. The partnership rapidly flourished, gaining a name as a principled manufacturer of high quality consumer goods sold at competitive prices. The Procter & Gamble Company was incorporated in 1890, and in every decade since incorporation, sales more than doubled. By 1992, P&G was a multinational company with annual sales of almost $30 billion (U.S.), profits exceeding $1.8 billion (U.S.), and a long-standing reputation for quality products, high integrity, strong marketing, and conservative management.

As Procter & Gamble grew, it increasingly focused on international markets. In 1992, P&G's brands were sold in more than 140 countries around the world. Major areas and representative brands included laundry and cleaning products (e.g., Tide, Cheer, Mr. Clean), paper products (Pampers, Luvs, Always, Bounty, Charmin), health care (Pepto-Bismol, Metamucil), oral care (Crest, Scope), food and beverage (Jif, Crisco), bar soaps (Ivory, Zest) and cosmetics (Oil Of Olay, Max Factor, Cover Girl). Many of these brands were leaders in their categories.

In Canada, P&G operated as Procter & Gamble Inc., with 1992 sales expected to exceed $1.7 billion, and earnings before taxes of over $100 million. P&G Inc. operated as four divisions, of which Paper Products was one, organized on a category basis within each division (e.g., Tissue/Towel/Facial within Paper Products).

Procter & Gamble in Paper Products

Procter & Gamble first entered the consumer paper market in 1957 with its acquisition of Charmin Paper Company, a regional company with a strong presence in the north central U.S. In the early 1960s, P&G developed proprietary papermaking technologies which allowed it to deliver softness, strength and absorbency that were superior to conventionally manufactured products. This technology was used to strengthen the Charmin toilet tissue brand, leading to national expansion in the mid-sixties. Simultaneously, P&G launched Bounty towels, also employing the new technology, and subsequently expanded the brand to national distribution in 1972. Finally, P&G entered the facial tissue market in the early 1970s by launching the Puffs brand, which was initially sold as a regional brand, then expanded to the national market in 1990.

P&G built Charmin, Bounty and Puffs with similar strategies. First, proprietary technology was used to deliver products with superior performance at a competitive price. As well, consumers were offered "value-added" products which delivered additional benefits (e.g., Puffs Plus with lotion, Charmin Free with no inks, dyes or perfumes). Third, the brands were supported with successful advertising themes and consistently high media weights.

Finally, P&G achieved competitive costs among premium brands by using Total Quality Methods to improve the papermaking process. Together, these strategies were extremely successful. Charmin and Bounty established clear market share leadership in their categories, with Puffs a close second (to Kimberly-Clark's Kleenex brand) in the facial tissue category.

The Facelle Acquisition

By 1991, P&G was sufficiently satisfied with its U.S. successes on Charmin, Bounty and Puffs that it was ready to take its first step in expanding the business. Canada was the logical first choice for that step, given its proximity to the U.S., the advent of free trade between Canada and the U.S., and the attendant opportunities for North American supply sourcing. At the time, P&G had only one paper plant in Canada, which manufactured diapers in Belleville, Ontario.

Early in 1991, an attractive acquisition opportunity developed for P&G. Canadian Pacific Forest Product Company, a large diversified paper company, was prepared to sell Facelle Paper Products, its tissue division. Facelle was a medium-sized manufacturer and marketer of tissue, towel and sanitary products, headquartered in Toronto. In 1990, Facelle reported an operating profit of $13.4 million on sales of $170.5 million. The deal was concluded in August 1991; for $185 million, P&G bought the Facelle Co., its plant in Toronto, and its franchise for facial tissue, paper towels and bathroom tissue, including the Royale, Florelle, Pronto, Dove, Facettes, and Festival brands.

THE CONSUMER PAPER BUSINESS IN CANADA

The Canadian consumer paper market in 1992 was about 25 million cases, where a case represented a shipping unit of approximately equivalent size for the three principal types of tissue. In the facial tissue category, a case contained the equivalent of 48 boxes of 150 two-ply tissues. Of the 25 million cases, bathroom tissue accounted for 13 million, paper towels seven million, and facial tissue five million. Tissue products were inexpensive (usually less than $2.00 per package), they were widely used (in more than 95 per cent of Canadian households), and they were frequently purchased (on average, once every two weeks). Brand switching was high, as there were many acceptable substitutes and the risk associated with product failure was low. The challenge for manufacturers was to differentiate their products enough on performance to build loyalty.

Retailing

Not surprisingly, retailers viewed paper as a low-profit, low-loyalty category, and they used it primarily to draw consumers into their stores. Traditional food stores typically carried a full line of paper products and featured them frequently. In recent years, however, mass merchandiser and drug chains had expanded their paper business substantially, focusing almost exclusively on price deals to attract customers to their stores. Recently, "club stores," with their emphasis on everyday low pricing, further squeezed retail and manufacturer margins. The vigorous retail competition had led to heavy featuring, where some brand was on sale virtually every week of the year, with resultant low profit margins. The challenge for manufacturers was to convince retailers to use their brands as the key feature items while trying to find ways to help retailers build profit.

Manufacturing

The paper business in Canada had a few very large national manufacturers and a few smaller regional players. This structure was driven, in part, by the sizable scale efficiencies that had been achieved in papermaking. Therefore, the industry was characterized by high capital and fixed costs. A single paper machine cost at least $100 million (U.S.), and at capacity it could satisfy about 10 per cent of the Canadian market.

This cost structure, combined with the consumer and retail customer behaviours described above, strongly encouraged paper manufacturers to run their machines near capacity to maximize their contribution. Thus, most manufacturers marketed broad product lines in an attempt to compete in all segments of the market and utilize as much capacity as possible. Also, they competed intensely for the product features which drove volume at the retail level. It was common in the industry for one manufacturer to market both premium and price brands in all three of the Tissue, Towel and Facial categories, to supply retailers with private label products in the same categories, and to sell to the commercial and institutional markets as well. Furthermore, many retailers had moved to a "bidding" process that allocated featured promotions to the manufacturer with the most lucrative retail spending program.

The largest players in the Canadian consumer paper business were Scott Paper and Kimberly-Clark, both subsidiaries of successful large U.S. paper companies. In addition, there were several small regional players, of whom the largest was Irving Paper, operating in the Maritimes.

THE FACIAL TISSUE MARKET IN CANADA

A cost structure that Beard could envision for a national manufacturer competing aggressively in the facial tissue market is presented in Exhibit 1, based on the cost information presented above. Over half of the variable manufacturing cost of facial tissue was the cost of wood pulp.

The size of the facial tissue market in 1991 was 4,894,000 cases shipped, up seven per cent over 1990 sales. Market shares of the major producers, indexed to 1990 shares, are presented in Table 1. They will be discussed in the following paragraphs.

TABLE 1	Facial Tissue Market Shares–1991	
Company/Brand	**Percentage Share of 1991 Shipments**	**Total P&G Index vs. 1990 Shares**
Royale	6.9	101[1]
Florelle[2]	5.8	67
Total P&G	12.7	84
Kimberly-Clark	39.5	107
Scott	23.0	88
Irving	4.2	n.a.
All Others	20.6	98
	100.0	

1. Index = (1991 share) / (1990 share) * 100. For example, the Royale index of 101 was calculated by dividing Royale's 1991 market share of 6.9 per cent by their share of 6.8 per cent in 1990.
2. In data throughout the case, Florelle numbers will include the Facettes brand. Facettes was a minor price brand.

Brand Developments in 1991

Facelle Brands. Shipments of the Facelle brands of facial tissue in 1991 were only 622,000 cases, or 84 per cent of the 1990 results. Two brands, Royale and Florelle, accounted for most of Facelle's sales. Florelle and Royale were made from the same base tissue stock, with Royale having three layers or plys, while Florelle had only two. Until recently, the Royale brand had been the only 3-ply tissue on the market, and it enjoyed a brand image as the traditional, strong, premium quality facial tissue. Its market share increased very slightly during 1991. Florelle was a 2-ply tissue that had received little promotional attention. Not surprisingly, it had low awareness, trial and image. It had lost about one-third of its market share in 1991, down to 5.8 per cent.

Kimberly-Clark. The Kleenex brand had enjoyed a very good year in 1991, gaining 2.5 share points to reach 39.5 per cent of units shipped in the Canadian market. In fact, Kleenex's share reached 41.7 per cent in the second half of the year. For several years in the late 1980s, Kimberly-Clark had made no significant changes in the Kleenex brand. However, there were several Kleenex product initiatives during 1991 which affected the brand's sales results. The new 300-tissue family size (2-ply) package, which had first been introduced in September 1989, had completed its national rollout in 1991; it achieved a share for the year of 8.2 per cent, up from 3.1 per cent in 1990. Also, the rollout of the 2-ply Kleenex 150, which replaced Kleenex 200s as the #1 stockkeeping unit (SKU) in the facial tissue category, was completed in 1991. Largely in support of this latter introduction, Kimberly-Clark increased merchandising support by 20 per cent in food retailers and 13 per cent in drug retailers. Finally, Kimberly-Clark introduced Kleenex Ultra, a 3-ply tissue which contained a silicone-based lotion, in the Ontario market in mid-1991. (Exhibits 2 and 3 show advertisements for Kleenex 150s and Ultra).

Scott. Scott's major brand, Scotties, fell from a share of 18.9 per cent in 1990 to 15.9 per cent in 1991. The main reason for the decline was the loss of trade support relative to Kleenex 150s. Scott relaunched the brand in September 1991, positioning it as a product with high content of recycled material, and supporting it with heavy advertising. (See Exhibit 4 for an example of Scotties' advertising.) As well, a 300-tissue family size of Scotties was launched in December 1991. Early indications were that the brand was recovering. Scott's secondary brand, White Swan (sold only in 150s), maintained a 7.1 per cent share in 1991. Increased merchandising in drug channels led to a share gain there, which compensated for the share loss in food channels in the face of Kleenex 150s with its stronger brand image.

Irving. Next to the aggressive developments in the Kleenex brand, the most significant competitive event in the facial tissue business in 1991 was the entry of Irving into the facial tissue market in the Maritime provinces and Quebec with its new Majesta brand. Majesta was packaged in an attractive format, and its feature pricing averaged 15 to 20 per cent below Kleenex. It achieved a 4.2 per cent national share in 1991.

All Others. Overall, the other brands in the Canadian marketplace retained 98 per cent of their cumulative market share in 1991. The group suffered some losses in the face of the merchandising support of Kleenex 150s, but these were balanced by gains in private label products in Western Canada.

Advertising

Advertising expenditures in the facial tissue category had historically been low, and quite inconsistent in "share of voice" and medium by manufacturer. Average industry annual expenditures were nearly $3.0 million over the last five years, with television accounting for 47 per cent of spending, "out-of-home" (i.e., billboards, posters, and mass transit ads) 32 per cent, consumer magazines 17 per cent and daily newspapers four per cent. Exhibit 5 summarizes copy and media strategy for the major brands in recent years, and share of advertising expenditures by brand.

Randall Beard believed that Kimberly-Clark had established a contemporary image for the Kleenex brand, but not a strong image for either softness or tissue strength. There had been no brand equity advertising[1] on the softness theme for the Kleenex brand since 1979, although there had been introductory campaigns for the softness upgrades to the basic product in 1989 and 1991, and the launch of the lotion line extension Kleenex Ultra in 1991.

Until the past year, when all Scotties' advertising was focused on the recycled paper relaunch behind an environmentally friendly position, Scotties had consistently advertised softness. This was somewhat ironic, because, according to P&G's tests of softness, the Scotties product was inferior on that dimension.

Royale had historically focused on the superior cold care afforded by the softness and strength of the 3-ply tissue. In 1991, ads for the product had emphasized softness, followed at year-end by the tactical cold season airing of an existing cold care execution.

By Procter & Gamble standards, advertising in the facial tissue category had not been strong. Not only were expenditures low, but only a small proportion of that spending was on brand equity. Furthermore, campaigns in the industry had tended to be of short duration, while P&G's extensive research on consumer advertising indicated that to be effective, advertising had to be sustained.

Consumer Promotion

Except for the Facelle brands, there was little consumer promotion activity in the category, relative to the norms for other consumer packaged goods. In 1991, the three major facial tissue suppliers ran a total of 35 consumer promotions, with 21 of those for the Facelle brands (13 for Royale and eight for Florelle, respectively). Of the 35 promotions, 19 were coupons, and the other 16 a variety of sweepstakes, mail-in offers, samples, and cross-coupons. Altogether, P&G estimated, the 19 coupon promotions moved an incremental 42,000 cases of product for the three brands, or less than one per cent of facial tissue shipments. In general, promotions did not pay for themselves because of the low absolute unit price of the product relative to the cost of the promotion. Therefore, promotions were likely to be used only as part of a more efficient group promotion, or as part of a strategy specifically directed at obtaining trial.

Pricing

While consumer promotions for facial tissues were relatively rare, price features were commonplace. There was always at least one brand on feature at any sizeable food or drug

---

1. Brand equity advertising builds the franchise and image of a brand; rather than merely providing information about a feature or an upgrade.

retailer. In fact, the vast majority of facial tissues sold at retail during 1991 were feature-priced. Typical prices for the major brands during 1991 are shown below.

TABLE 2	Typical Prices–1991				
Brand	**Ply**	**Count**	**Typical Shelf Price**	**Typical Feature Price**	
P&G					
Royale	3	100	1.19	.89	
Florelle	2	200	1.09	.79	
Kimberley-Clark					
Kleenex	2	150	.99	.79	
Kleenex	2	300	1.99	1.59	
Kleenex-Ultra	3	100	.99	.79	
Scott					
Scotties	2	150	.99	.69	
Scotties	2	300	1.99	1.49	
White Swan	2	150	.89	.59	
Irving					
Majesta	2	150	.89	.63	
Private Labels	2	150	.79	.49	

ISSUES FOR THE FACELLE BRANDS

In planning the future of the Facelle brands, several problems had to be confronted. But first, Randall Beard reviewed a summary of the research which P&G had obtained in the seven months since acquiring the Facelle business.

The Royale Brand

Brand Image

Royale's long-term premium positioning, based upon its historically unique 3-ply product design and its softness claim, had built the leading brand image among its users in the product category. In judgments by a brand's users, Royale received an overall score of 85 on a scale of 100, marginally superior to Kleenex (at an average score of 82) and Scotties (81), and considerably ahead of the store brands (averaging 69).

Exhibit 6 compares four leading brands on a number of specific attributes of image. Royale enjoyed an image advantage for strength and thickness versus all other competition, but an image weakness for package design. Furthermore, it was seen as less fashionable than Kleenex and Scotties. The image data were particularly interesting to Beard and his product managers; despite low advertising spending in the category, historic campaigns appeared to have had a strong impact on brand image. For example, Scotties had a strong image for softness despite clearly inferior physical characteristics on that dimension relative to Royale and Kleenex. Almost ten years of advertising using the Little Softie character and the message "Scotties softens the blow" had evidently produced a strong image for the brand as a soft, gentle tissue that was good for sore nose care.

Although Royale enjoyed a very favourable overall brand image, knowledge about the brand was not as high as Beard would have expected. For instance, among those who had used it in the past three months, 47 per cent thought that Royale was a 2-ply tissue, and only 48 per cent correctly assessed it as 3-ply.

Product Usage

Although Royale enjoyed a very favourable overall brand image, that image did not translate to market share, as the table below demonstrates. Although half of households had used Royale sometime in the last year, only 14 per cent claimed that it was their usual brand over the past three months. Qualitative research indicated that Royale was used as a part-time brand that was bought on feature or specifically for cold care, but seldom for regular usage around the household. This pattern was confirmed by the image data which showed significantly less agreement with the statement "is inexpensive" for Royale (32 per cent) than Kleenex (52 per cent), Scotties (42 per cent), or store brands (83 per cent).

TABLE 3	Trial and Usage by Brand			
	Per Cent Usage by Brand			
	Royale	Kleenex	Scotties	Store Brands
1991 Market Share	6.9	39.5	15.9	20.6
Past 12 months used	51	91	52	29
Past 3 months used	34	79	33	22
Past 3 months usual brand	14	55	19	19
Loyalty: Used only this brand past 3 months	13	34	17	18
Share of total facial tissue usage past 12 months (among users of the brand)	14	45	36	80

Furthermore, as the following Table below shows, Royale usage was heavily skewed to older consumers and smaller households.

Table 4	Demographic Characteristics by Brand		
	Usual Brand		
Age Group	**Royale %**	**Kleenex %**	**Scotties %**
<24	3	5	2
25-50	48	68	63
>50	_49_	_27_	_35_
	100	100	100
Household Size			
1	16	10	8
2	42	32	35
>2	_42_	_58_	_57_
	100	100	100

Pricing vs. Kleenex

In the past, when the #1 SKU in the category was Kleenex 200s, feature price at retail on that product had been $0.99. Now, with the introduction of Kleenex 150s, feature price had dropped to $0.79, and sometimes lower in special promotions. In fact, in the past four months, average feature price for Kleenex had been $0.69, and for Royale $0.73. During this period, 80 per cent of the Royale sold at retail had been on feature. In the longer term, P&G estimated that the typical feature price for Kleenex 150s would be likely to increase modestly, but not dramatically. Furthermore, data from recent comparisons of Royale share at different levels of price disparity with Kleenex indicated higher price elasticity for Royale when its price exceeded Kleenex's by more than $.20.

Royale Price vs. Kleenex ($)	-.10	0.0	+.10	+.20	+.30	+.40
Royale Market Share (%)	7.2	7.0	6.8	6.2	5.2	4.1

The Florelle Brand

In 1991, 80 per cent of facial tissue units sold were standard 2-ply tissue, the segment in which Facelle was represented by the Florelle brand. Specialty sizes (e.g., pocket packs, man-size, and cube format) represented eight per cent of units, and 3-ply tissue about 12 per cent.

The table below presents data from a November 1991 panel study of 2215 households on their attitudes toward brands of facial tissue. Only three per cent of those surveyed claimed that Florelle was their usual brand. Not surprisingly for a brand which had received no advertising or consumer promotion, ratings of Florelle were not high.

TABLE 5	Brand Attitudes			
	All Users		**Past 3 Months Brand Users**	
Brand	**Average Value Rating**	**Average Overall Rating**	**% Who Purchased in Past 3 Months**	**Average Overall Rating**
Florelle	53	58	10	73
Royale	71	78	30	85
Kleenex	73	80	75	82
Scotties	68	74	29	81
White Swan	61	66	14	77
Majesta	49	55	8	75
Store Brand	53	56	17	69

The obvious alternatives were to drop the Florelle brand, rejuvenate it with support, or continue it as an unsupported price brand.

The Softness Issue

A key success factor in the successful development of the Puffs brand in the United States was the effort that P&G invested in making the tissue softer. Softness is influenced by the process used in manufacturing the tissue, and the type of fibre employed. Longer fibres tend to make the resultant tissue stronger, but not as soft; shorter fibres, like eucalyptus, produce a softer tissue. A key issue in manufacturing facial tissue, therefore, is how the softness/strength tradeoff is managed.

Data from P&G's experience in the U.S. market indicated that consumer preference as a function of strength followed an S-curve, where additional strength above the functional level did not provide any additional consumer benefit. On the other hand, softness did not level off in terms of diminishing returns on customer perceptions—at least at the levels of softness which could currently be obtained.

Relative tissue strength depended upon the conditions of the test, especially whether the tissue was wet or dry. A given brand of tissue, which had much higher dry strength than a second brand, would not necessarily have much higher wet strength. Procter & Gamble believed that dry strength (which affected ease of dispensing the tissue) was much less important than wet strength (which directly affected consumers' use of the product).

The data below show wet burst strength and softness for leading brands in the Canadian market. Softness was measured through tactile judgments of a panel of consumers, using Puffs as the standard zero-point on the scale.

TABLE 6	Softness and Strength of Leading Brands of Facial Tissue	
Brand	Softness[1]	Wet Burst Strength (g/sheet)
Royale	-2.5	69
Florelle	-2.1	32
Kleenex	-1.1	31
Kleenex Ultra	-0.5	76
Scotties	-2.0	57

[1] On this scale, Puffs tissues are rated at 0. Differences of 0.5 scale points or more are considered to be noticeable.

Commenting on this data, Randall Beard said, "This just reinforces what I have been told about Facelle's strategy prior to the acquisition. They chose to maximize strength—particularly dry strength—but that approach cost them severely on the softness dimension."

A study of customer dissatisfaction asked participants whether, in the past three months, they had experienced a problem with tissue breaking. Only one per cent of Royale users had experienced a problem, vs. seven per cent of Kleenex users.

In mid-1991, a blind paired comparison test was conducted with Royale and Kleenex Ultra. Attribute ratings on strength were the same for the two brands (8.5 on a 10-point scale), but Kleenex Ultra was rated significantly better on softness (9.1 vs. 7.4). When asked which brand they preferred overall, only 27 per cent of participants chose Royale.

Beard was convinced that P&G needed to upgrade the softness of the Facelle products. By adding eucalyptus fibre and sacrificing some tissue strength, their softness could be significantly improved without the need for a major capital expenditure. In the long run, investments in process improvement could produce further softness enhancements, but the so-called "Eucalyptus Upgrade" could be done in a few months for a modest investment.

Accordingly, P&G carried out a pilot project to produce enough of the upgraded products for consumer acceptance testing. Early in 1992, "Single Product Blind Tests" (SPBT) were completed on the upgraded product, in both 2-ply and 3-ply form, as well as the current Royale, Florelle, Kleenex (Regular and Ultra), Scotties, and White Swan. In a SPBT, a sample of facial tissue with no identifying features is sent to a participant, who then uses the product for several weeks and answers a questionnaire about it. Participants in Facelle's SPBT were female heads of households whose first language was English. There were eight groups of participants, one for each brand. Group sizes ranged from 259 to 280 individuals. Results of this study are presented in Exhibit 7.

Overall ratings of the brands were found to be a function of consumer impressions of a tissue's softness and its thickness. A multiple regression with these two independent variables explained more than 95 per cent of the variation in overall rating scores. The resultant equation is presented below:

$$\text{Overall Rating} = 19.51 + (0.424 * \text{Softness Rating}) + (0.359 * \text{Thickness Rating})$$

One issue in introducing an upgraded tissue was its perception by current Royale and Kleenex users. Would a new 2-ply product cannibalize sales of 3-ply Royale, or would it take share from Kleenex? Would a new 3-ply product be seen as an improvement by users of the current Royale tissue? Exhibit 8 compares ratings of the upgraded products by users of Royale and Kleenex, respectively, with similar users' ratings of the existing Royale and Florelle products. It is noteworthy that current Royale users who received the 2-ply upgrade in the SPBT were less favourably impressed with it than a group who actually received Royale in the blind test. In other words, the improved softness of the upgrade did not offset the reduction from three plies to two. The exhibit also enables a comparison of the group who received the 3-ply upgrade with the one that received current Royale in the blind tests. In that situation, current Royale users rated the upgrade significantly higher on softness, slightly lower on strength and somewhat more favourably overall.

If the 2-ply upgrade were to be introduced, Randall Beard had to make a decision about what brand name would be used on it. Two apparent alternatives were Florelle (as an upgrade of the existing brand) and Royale (as a line extension). Furthermore, if the Royale name were chosen, a decision would have to be made about how to distinguish the 2-ply upgrade from the 3-ply upgrade of the traditional Royale brand. Another possibility would be to introduce the new product under the Puffs label that had been so successfully launched in the U.S. some twenty years earlier. Although Puffs had never been sold in Canada, there had been enough advertising spill-in from the U.S. that the brand was known to some Canadians. The table below shows data on the image of Puffs among English and French Canadians.

TABLE 7	Canadian Consumer Evaluations of the Puffs Brand			
	English HHs		**French HHs**	
	Royale %	**Puffs** %	**Royale** %	**Puffs** %
Awareness	97	40	97	11
TV Adv. Awareness	36	18	33	3
Trial (past 12 mos.)	51	9	57	3
Overall Rating	82	57	84	37
Judgment of Value	66	48	72	39
Of Those Aware				
% agreeing that the brand is good for nose care	42	77	30	33

CONCLUSION

Using the Puffs label in Canada would be a step toward making Puffs a North American brand, an alternative which would certainly have the blessing of the U.S. parent. However, the primary responsibility for the decision rested with Randall Beard and Barbara Fraser, and the choice had to be made soon if product, packaging and advertising and merchandising programs were to be ready for the fall cold season.

"This is the year that we have to begin our move to make Facelle a major player in the market," said Randall Beard to himself, "and there are a number of issues we must face. Our long-term goal is a profitable leading share of the market, which is a long way from where we are now. To get there, it is essential that we establish a winning strategy for the Facelle Division brands." To do so, Beard felt, several inter-related questions had to be answered. What should be done about the Florelle brand? Should available technology from P&G be employed to increase the softness of Royale? What should be the position of the Facelle brand in the 2-ply segment? In fact, what brand should Facelle employ in that segment—and Puffs, or an altogether new brand?

EXHIBIT 1	Typical Cost Structure: Facial Tissue in Canada	
		Cost per Case of 48 Units of 150-count two-ply tissue
Net Revenue		$54
Off-invoice Allowance	$9[1]	
Co-op Allowance	10[2]	
Less: Total Discounts and Allowance		19
Net Sales		35
Less: Variable Manufacturing Cost (Including Delivery)		16[3]
Contribution		19
Manufacturing Fixed Cost	11	
Selling, Research, & Administration	3	
Marketing Support[4]	1	
Less: Total Fixed Costs		15
Profit		$4

1. Average price reduction through the year, assuming feature price reductions of 25 per cent were given on approximately 2/3 of the unit volume.
2. Allowance for co-operative advertising and promotion. Some of these funds were actually used by retailers for this purpose, and the rest was retained by them.
3. In March 1992, about 55 per cent of the variable manufacturing cost of facial tissue was the cost of wood pulp. As a result, there was a substantial difference in profitability between the Florelle and Royale brands.
4. Advertising, couponing, sampling. For many of the existing brands, less than $1 per case was spent on advertising support.

EXHIBIT 2	Example of Kleenex 150s Ad

Kleenex Tissues	Feb 17, 91
523-03	CBUT
30 seconds	Vancouver

(Music throughout)

ANNCR (VO): What do the experts think of new softer Kleenex Tissues.

BABY 1: I been waitin', waitin' so long…

BABY 2 & 3: Bee-doo-bee-doo…

BABY 4 …for you to come along.

BABY 2 &3: …bee-doo-bee-doo…

BABY 5: Softer.

ANNCR (VO): New Kleenex Tissues are even softer now. Made with soft

natural fibres. They're baby soft.

BABY 3: …bee-doo-bee…

BABY 3: …come softly…

BABY 4: …darling.

SINGERS: Softer than ever.

BABY 5: Softer.

BABY 2& 3: Da-bee-doo…

(Fades out)

EXHIBIT 3	Example of Kleenex Ultra Ad

Kleenex Ultra Tissues: Lotion Bottle

30 seconds

ANNCR (VO): Kleenex Ultra tissues with lotion.

So it feels soft and soothing

on even the sorest nose.

Kleenex Ultra

Softer, because it has lotion.

EXHIBIT 4	Example of Scotties Ad

The Same Tissue That's Pampering Your Cold This Year, Just Might Have
Been A Get Well Card Last Year.

That may sound like a far fetched notion. But in reality it could
happen. That's because consumers like you wanted a facial tissue safe
for the environment, yet soft enough for their skin. Scott Paper
responded with Scotties Recycled. It still has that famous Scotties
softness you've come to depend on, only now its made from more than two
thirds recycled paper. Which makes Scotties Recycled the natural
choice for softness.

Scott

We Care About The Same Things You Do.

EXHIBIT 5	Advertising Strategy of Facial Tissue Competitors

A. Copy Strategy

Brand	Years	Copy Strategy—Execution	Medium
Kleenex	1980-88	Heritage - family moments	TV, Print
		New packaging - pack shot	Print
	1989-91	Improved softness	TV
		Lotion - demonstration	TV, Print, OOH[1]
Scotties	1967-89	Softest cold care - "Scotties soften the blow"	TV
	1990	Caring softness - "Softer than a kiss"	TV
	1991	Environmentally friendly	Print, OOH
Royale	1973-86	Superior cold care - 3-ply softness and strength	TV
	1988-90	New packaging	OOH
	1991	"Kitteny soft"	TV
	1992	Superior cold care - 3-ply	
		demonstration	TV

1. OOH indicates advertising message delivered Outside Of Home (e.g. through billboards or mass transit advertising).

B. Share of Advertising Expenditure

Brand	Share of Advertising Spending			
	1988	1989	1990	1991
Royale	25%	52%	49%	16%
Kleenex	2%	35%	15%	18%
Kleenex Ultra	—	—	—	21%
Scotties	50%	13%	25%	33%
White Swan	3%	—	10%	6%
Majesta	—	—	1%	6%
Other	20%	—	—	—
TOTAL	100%	100%	100%	100%

EXHIBIT 6	Brand Images by Attribute[1]

| | Brand Rating | | | |
Attribute	Royale	Kleenex	Scotties	Store Brands
• is soft	0	–	+	–
• good for sore nose care	0	0	+	–
• does not tear or fall apart when I blow my nose or sneeze	+	0	0	0
• is absorbent	+	–	0	0
• is thick	+	–	–	–
• contains lotion	0	+	0	0
• is 3-ply	+	–	–	0
• design/colours on box are attractive	–	+	+	–
• is caring	0	0	+	0
• is fashionable	–	+	0	–
• is contemporary	–	0	0	0
• is inexpensive	–	–	–	+

1. In this chart, 0 represents a score that was not different from the average rating for all brands, - a score that was lower than the average rating, and + a score that was higher.

EXHIBIT 7	Consumer Evaluations of Facial Tissues in SPBT[1]

Brand	Overall[2]	Softness	Strength	Thickness	Absorbency
Facelle					
Royale:					
• current	82[3]	78	91	87	85
• 3-ply upgrade	88	93	90	87	85
Florelle:					
• current	73	70	74	68	70
• 2-ply upgrade	80	89	73	72	75
Kleenex					
Regular	75	82	68	65	71
Ultra	90	94	89	87	86
Scott					
Scotties	63	58	66	58	63
White Swan	62	50	74	63	65

1. Ratings of English-speaking female heads of household, on a scale of 0-100 based on a single product blind test (SPBT) in home.
2. Each respondent was asked: "Considering everything about the facial tissue sent to you, how would you rate it OVERALL?"
3. For this sample size, differences of more than 5 scale points across groups (i.e., within a column in the table) are significant at the .05 level.

EXHIBIT 8	SPBT[1] Ratings of Current Facelle Products and the Upgrades							
	Users of Royale in Past 3 Months				Users of Kleenex in Past 3 Months			
Attribute Ratings	**3-ply Upgrade**	**Current Royale**	**2-Ply Upgrade**	**Current Florelle**	**3-ply Upgrade**	**Current Royale**	**2-ply Upgrade**	**Current Florelle**
Overall	90	83	77	72	89	81	80	74
Softness	94	77	89	72	93	76	90	70
Strength	89	83	68	72	90	91	74	76
Thickness	90	88	68	63	88	86	72	69
Absorbency	87	85	74	69	86	84	75	71

1. Single Product Blind Test ratings. Each column in the table represents ratings by a group who received the indicated product in a blind test. Differences across columns of 6 scale points or more are statistically significant at the .05 level.

BALLYGOWAN SPRINGS INTO NEW AGE KISQUA

Brenda Cullen[1]

In January 1991 Geoff Read, managing director of Ballygowan Spring Water Company, had to make a decision that could alter the whole direction of the company. Since August 1988 the management team had shaped a strategy to launch a drink to develop upon the success of Ballygowan Spring Water. The objective was to provide Ballygowan with a product to enter the soft-drinks market and so remove the weakness of being a one-product company. After identifying the market for 'new age' products, and carrying out research at each stage in the product development process, the results of a final test market were disappointing. Ballygowan had to consider whether to withdraw the product, to redesign and reposition the new range or to go ahead and launch as originally planned.

Ballygowan

Geoff Read founded Ballygowan in 1981. Initially the idea of selling bottled water to the Irish consumer met with scepticism from the banks. However, by 1991 Ballygowan exported to 15 countries and held 77 per cent of the 12.5 million litre water market in Ireland and had developed an extensive range of bottled spring water products.

Between 1987 and 1989 the company grew to be a medium-sized enterprise geared for expansion and growth. A joint investment with Anheuser Busch provided a very modern production facility covering 270,000 square feet with a capacity of 600 bottles per minute. Ballygowan's success came from being an innovator in the market for water-based products, and also from astute management of the Ballygowan brand franchise. Management now saw the need to exploit the asset of the company more profitably. In particular the plant

---

1. University College Dublin, Ireland.

was not at full capacity and the company's strong distribution network and experienced management were not being fully utilized.

Bottled water market

By the end of 1985 the bottled water market in Ireland was I£1.2 million[2] (2.8 million litres) with about 10 per cent of adults drinking mineral water regularly. By 1990 it had grown to I£12.5 million (12.5 million litres), about 5.5 per cent of the Irish soft drinks market (see Exhibit 6.1). The bottled water market was 'one of the fastest growing sectors in the food trade in both Ireland and the UK'. Reasons for this were reduction in the quality of tap water, and changing attitudes towards health and fitness, which led to an increase in the demand for drinks perceived as natural, alcohol free and with fewer calories. Furthermore, *increasingly* stringent drink-driving legislation was leading to an increase in the consumption of bottled water. A Euromonitor survey in 1989 showed that the Irish consumed far less bottled water per person than other countries (Ireland: 3 litres; United Kingdom: 5.5; Italy: 80; Germany: 76; France: 68; and the United States: 30).

The market potential for spring water in Ireland was small considering the number of competitor brands on the market (see Exhibit 6.2). While some niche brands had high prices, low prices were becoming common because of aggressive high-street pricing, own-label products, and cheap imports. With a proliferation of products and the threat of commoditization it was becoming difficult to develop new niches in the market.

Ballygowan Spring Water

Ballygowan's success came from the sparkling and non-sparkling waters—Ballygowan Sparkling Irish Spring Water and Ballygowan Natural Irish Spring Water. A later addition to the range was Ballygowan Light, and in 1988 Ballygowan successfully launched a range of flavoured spring waters. By 1990 the company's turnover was I£10 million, a figure they hoped to double within the next two years. An important part of this strategy was the launch of soft drinks, a market where the company saw significant volume potential.

EXHIBIT 6.1	Irish bottled water market: segment growth		
Year	Still lit./m.	Sparkling lit./m.	Petillant lit./m.
1988	28%	72%	—
1989	34%	66%	—
1990	33%	65%	2%

---

2. 1 ecu = US$1.26 = Dr.302 (Greek drachmas).

EXHIBIT 6.2	Dominant brands in the Irish bottled water market (% volume)			
Year	Ballygowan	Tipperary	Perrier	Other
1987	75.0	9.5	13.0	2.5
1988	76.0	11.0	8.0	5.0
1989	77.0	12.8	7.0	3.2
1990	78.0	13.5	4.0	4.5

Source: A.C. Nielsen.

The management wanted to launch a new drink to bring Ballygowan further into the mainstream soft-drinks market. It would enhance the company's reputation for innovation, market leadership, excellence and product quality. The product would be purer, juicier, fruitier and healthier than any other soft drink on the market. The brand should be consistent with developing consumer behaviour, particularly attitudes and behaviours towards healthy diets and lifestyles.

The Irish carbonated soft-drinks market in 1990 was about 235 million litres including approximately 40 million litres of adult soft drinks (see Exhibit 6.3). Soft-drink consumers were the target market for the proposed new product. They were likely to be more adult than young and would prefer to drink 7-Up or Club Orange to Coke or Pepsi. The profile of this consumer was 'a sophisticated, self-righteous and reasonably health-conscious adult', 18–30 years old, who wants and will pay for drinks which look good, taste good and portray a certain image.

EXHIBIT 6.3	Irish carbonated drinks market	
Year	Litres (m.)	Increase on previous year (%)
1987	179	7
1988	195	9
1989	224	15
1990 (estimated)	285	27
1991 (projected)	320	12
Packaging 1990	**Share of total market (%)**	**Litres (m.)**
Glass returnable	26	46.0
Glass nonreturnable	8	23.0
Pet	55	157.0
Cans	19	54.0
Disposable	3	7.0
Total	100	287.0

Flavour analysis 1990	Share of total market (%)
Lemonade (inc. 7-Up)	38
Cola	24
Orange	25
Tonic-mixer	8
Other	5

Source: SDDB&A

A product development process identified product development, brand development and business planning stages. The Ballygowan company employed a marketing consultancy firm to help in the first two stages.

Product Development Process

In December 1988 Ballygowan instructed Dimension, a marketing consultancy. The consultancy's brief was:

- Identify and brief three companies to develop prototype products based on pure juices and Ballygowan Spring Water with natural flavours and sweeteners, carbonated, containing preservatives, but not pasteurized.
- Develop formulations for up to six flavours.
- Develop name, branding, positioning, communication and marketing strategies.
- Target the branded soft-drink sector—Coke, 7-Up, Club, Lilt, and so on.
- Develop a brand with a premium but accessible imagery, and superior product quality but priced competitively with major brands.
- The brand should have no overt Ballygowan endorsement.
- Packed in 1.5 litre plastic bottles, 330 ml. cans, 250 ml. glasses.
- Primary focus to be the Irish market, but with export potential.

Product Sourcing

The first task was to find a company that could manufacture the pure fruit juice to mix with Ballygowan Spring Water. Criteria for the selection of a company were degree of technological sophistication, ability to produce a range of flavours, expertise in producing fruit juices and flavours, product quality, hygiene standards and speed of response. Three short-listed companies were briefed. Visits to each company appraised their production processes and capabilities.

The three companies each made laboratory-scale products, which were tested using a structured questionnaire assessing aroma, appearance, taste and overall opinion on each of the test products. All tests were 'blind', and the products were compared with successful brands already on the market as 'controls'. The range of flavours screened included orange, lemon, apple, passion fruit, grapefruit, peach, pineapple, blackberry and blackcurrant. The aim was to achieve product ratings competitive with the 'controls' (see Exhibit 6.4).

After the analysis of each batch, the three companies were rebriefed, shown the taste test results and told the changes required. After repeating the process six times a German company, which responded particularly well to the product brief and to the taste tests, was appointed as the supplier. Both companies then agreed plant and equipment specifications.

Product Formulations

Six products were produced for a quantitative market research survey conducted in May 1989 by Behaviour and Attitudes, a market research agency in Dublin. A questionnaire, developed from Dimension's earlier one, focused on aroma, appearance and flavour. The flavours tested were 10 per cent orange juice, 15 per cent orange peach juice, 15 per cent orange passion fruit juice, 10 per cent orange lemon juice, 10 per cent lemon juice, and 15 per cent grapefruit and pineapple juice, with Club Orange and Club Lemon as 'controls'. Each of 200 respondents taste-tested two Ballygowan samples and one of the 'controls', to give 75 assessments of each Ballygowan product.

EXHIBIT 6.4	Taste test				
Product	**Aroma***	**Appearance***	**Taste***	**Overall score**	**Likelihood of purchase****
Club Orange	6.9	7.5	7.3	7.4	3.5
Dohler Orange	5.9	5.6	6.1	6.1	2.6
Dohler Orange and Peach	7.4	7.2	7.1	7.5	3.3
Dohler Orange and Passion Fruit	6.6	6.3	7.0	7.0	3.2
Dohler Orange and Lemon	6.4	6.4	6.9	7.2	3.2
Club Lemon	6.7	6.5	7.2	7.4	3.5
Dohler Lemon	6.5	6.9	6.9	7.4	3.2
Dohler Grapefruit and Pineapple	5.8	6.2	5.5	6.1	2.5

Note: *Average scores on nine-point scale, in which 9 = most favourable and 1 = least favourable; ** on a scale of 1 to 5.
Source: Dimension, March 1989.

The results convinced the Ballygowan team to focus on orange, orange and peach, orange and passion fruit, and orange and lemon. Lemon, and grapefruit and pineapple, could extend the range later (see Exhibit 6.5). Since the results of the orange formulation were not satisfactory a second round of quantitative market research would take place with performance isolated from packaging and advertising effects.

Some questions remained. Should the products be pasteurized, and should essence or preservatives be used? Each of these options had complications. Pasteurization meant that it would not be possible to use plastic bottles and there were also shelf-life implications. However, with pasteurization, the product ingredients are '100 per cent natural'. Using essence would overcome shelf-life difficulties but their use would not be consistent with the brand propositions. Finally, preservatives were in most soft drinks on the market but the management felt that they could compromise Ballygowan's image of purity and naturalness.

Product Concept and Brand Name Development

The development of the product concept and branding began with brainstorming sessions by Dimension, Ballygowan's specification for the name was that it should be relevant, attractive, distinctive, memorable, registerable and have the attributes of a global brand name. Out of the hundreds of names generated Juisca, Juzze, Artesia, Kisqua, Prima, and Viva became prototype brand names. Five positioning options also helped explore the attitudes and motivations of soft-drink consumers:

1. *Health drink.* A pure, natural and healthy drink for mainstream soft-drink consumers who care about what they consume.

2. *Sophisticated.* A high status drink of superior quality for discerning consumers.

3. *Healthy lifestyle.* For those who unselfconsciously lead and aspire to a healthy but full lifestyle in terms of diet, exercise and a relaxed but full life.

4. *Youthful peer groupies.* The Pepsi/Club generation.

5. *Generic.* Refreshment, cooling, youthful and Coke sociability values.

EXHIBIT 6.5	Summary ratings							
	Orange peach (15% juice)	Orange lemon (10% juice)	Club orange	Orange (10% juice)	Orange passion fruit (15% juice)	Lemon (10% juice)	Club lemon	Grapefruit and pineapple (15% juice)
Aroma								
Attractiveness	5	3	4	2	3	4	4	2
Naturalness	5	2	2	2	4	3	3	2
Overall	5	3	3	2	3	4	4	2
Appearance								
Attractiveness	4	2	5	1	3	5	2	3
Naturalness	5	3	4	1	3	5	3	3
Overall	5	3	5	2	3	5	4	2
Flavour								
Good taste	4	3	5	1	3	4	5	1
Real fruit flavour	5	3	3	1	4	5	3	1
Sweetness (right)	5	3	3	3	3	5	5	3
Refreshment	5	3	5	1	3	5	5	1
Overall taste	5	3	4	1	4	4	4	1
Overall rating	5	4	4	1	3	4	5	1

Key: 5 Well above average
 4 Above average
 3 Average
 2 Below average
 1 Well below average

Source: Behaviour and Attitudes, Market Research Survey, May 1989.

A market research agency, Behaviour & Attitudes, designed and conducted four focus groups representing market segments with different relationship to soft drinks (see Exhibit 6.6). The focus groups aimed to:

- Investigate the response to five prototype brand names.
- Explore reaction to seven prototype pack designs.
- Consider pack designs and bottling formats.
- Give direction to brand positioning.

Discussions with each group followed a similar pattern. Initially respondents freely discussed their use and purchase of soft drinks. This naturally led to conversations about different brands. Next, the groups were told about the new idea for a soft drink and shown a board illustrating the new product concept. Following their responses to the concept the groups were told that there were alternative prototype brand names and packaging designs. These were presented one by one, with the order of presentation being rotated between different groups. Proposed brand names and pack designs were presented separately.

Later, discussion group members were asked to help market the new brand; 'mood boards' were presented and associated with the different brand names and pack designs. Finally, copy statements, presented on boards representing different positioning options, were discussed.

In September 1989, Behaviour and Attitudes debriefed Ballygowan about the research. First, they presented consumer attitudes to soft drinks generally (see Exhibit 6.7). The research indicated that teenage men, teenage girls and young married women had different attitudes and motivations to soft drinks. Secondly, they examined consumer attitudes to soft-drink brands (see Exhibit 6.8) and consumer reaction to the five prototype brands (see Exhibit 6.9). Behaviour & Attitudes made the following points about reactions to the product concepts:

1. The ingredients make it more sophisticated than mainstream soft drinks.
2. It was not seen as a totally novel idea. Consumers were aware of Nashs, Citrus Spring and Britvic.
3. The pleasant product and the endorsement of Ballygowan aroused a high predisposition to try it.
4. Price parity with Coke and 7-Up raised consumers' disposition to try the product.

A series of meetings between Dimension and the Ballygowan management team considered brand positioning and target market strategies. They chose Kisqua as the brand name. It was stylish, novel, distinctive, memorable, appropriate, warm and had the attributes of a world brand name. Ballygowan also applied for registration of Artesia in case the company should wish to launch an up-market spring water.

EXHIBIT 6.6   Focus groups

The four groups were:

1. Young teenage girls   Middle class
2. Young men   18-24 C_1C_2
3. Women   22-32 C_2 with children
4. Women   22-32 B_1B_2 with children

Target markets

Primary	Secondary
Health/body conscious ABC1 Late teens/twenties Young and early teens Teenage adults	Soft-drink consumers

Source: Behaviour & Attitudes, Market Research, August 1989.

Marketing Mix

The Ballygowan company next needed to know the impact of the brand name, label design, price, positioning and advertising options on Kisqua's branding strategy. A further question was the reason for people's preference for Kisqua or Club Orange. In October 1989 Behaviour and Attitudes researched these key areas. They used a central location to approach a quota sample of 200 respondents. The respondents were in two equal subgroups: one group to taste-test Club Orange and Kisqua blind, and the other group with both products branded. The results in percentages were:

	Blind	Branded
Prefer Club a lot	59	39
Prefer Club a little	16	19
Prefer Kisqua a lot	19	0
Prefer Kisqua a little	6	6
No preferences	6	3

EXHIBIT 6.7	General consumer attitudes to soft drinks	
Young men	**Young girls**	**Young married women**
• Perceived as the province of children and teenagers • Believe they are not emotionally involved in the market • Yet they are regular consumers—for thirst/refreshment • Therefore taste and refreshment are their criteria for judging soft drinks • Coca-Cola is the preferred brand • They associate 7-Up with contemporary youth and refreshment • Will be difficult to impress—little emotional interest in soft drinks.	• Very involved with brands as badges of both individuality and groups • Very conscious of style and fashion • Very high level of health consciousness • Brands reflect social valuations and status—Ballygowan, Perrier and 7-Up are stylish, sophisticated and healthy • Are high-volume users of soft drinks	• Regular purchasers for themselves and their families • Soft drinks are an essential household purchase item • Oriented towards health and exercise, and reflected in their attitude to food and drink brands • Disposed towards natural products, and low-calorie products • 'Natural' products identified as contemporary and fashionable • Working class want brands to be accessible—middle class focus on style

EXHIBIT 6.8   Consumer attitudes to soft-drink brands

Coke
• Perceived as the archetypal soft drink.
• Strong consistent branding, massive advertising support.
• Two problems: perceived by some as harsh causing tooth decay, overly masculine personality.

Club Orange
• The archetypal orange soft drink.
• Its appeal is primarily based on its product characteristics—real orange taste with lots of orange in it.
• Advertising not consistent with the brand.

Lilt
• Has no clear product focus—a mix of different things.
• Dissonance between advertising and product knowledge.

7-Up
• Very coherent brand, with well-rounded persona.
• Very popular and the most contemporary soft drink.

• 'The soft drink for the 1990s.'
• Healthy perception—clean and clear.
• Appeals to male and female.
• Not limited to teenagers: helped by its mixer usage; helped by its healthy image.
• Strong perception of being refreshed.

Club Lemon
• Valued for its product characteristics of taste and refreshment.
• Very loyal consumers—almost a cult.

Lucozade
• Strong healthy drink imagery.
• Regarded as a soft drink by young men.
• Well out of its old hospital/sick bed positioning.
• Reparative quality for handling hangovers.

EXHIBIT 6.9	Consumer reactions to five prototype brands	

Prototype brand	Reaction to name	Reaction to design
Artesia	• Distinctive but difficult to come to terms with. • Far too up-market/exclusive. • Not appropriate to the product concept. • Will not appeal to a mass market. • More relevant to wine.	• Very up-market, albeit very beautiful. • Very designery, 'yuppie' and exclusive. • Very aspirational. • Very distinctive, but so sophisticated as to exclude the large majority.
Prima	• Very favourably received by working class—very easy to empathize with. • Straightforward, direct and impactful for the working class. • Targeted at mass market—no pretensions. • But, rejected by middle class. • Just another name, pedestrian. • Little depth of imagery. • Association with Pennys gives it a downmarket image. • No distinctiveness.	• Appealed only to a small minority, and contemporary. • Otherwise perceived as oriented to very young children. • Very dissonant with product concept.
Viva	• Strong appeal to teenage girls—they associated it with beauty, fashion and style. • International—but cliché and pedestrian. • Strong negative Spanish association: cheap Spanish orange drink; 'Viva España'; Costa del Sol. • Lively, bright, extrovert and exuberant. • Dynamic and modern brand.	• Lacked novelty, not stylish, not sophisticated. • Cheap. • Dissonant with the Ballygowan heritage. • Looked Spanish—negative imagery. • Blue colour not liked.
Juzze	• Significant pronunciation difficulties. • Superficial and artificial. • Yet youthful, contemporary and up to date. • International. • Correlated with the product concept, except for a phoniness in its spelling. • Associated with zest, zing and vitality. • Suggested pure fruit juice.	• In mainstream of soft-drinks market. • Very OK, but no surprise, or aspirational qualities. • Lacks excitement or fun, too logical. • Consistently compared with Squeez and Britvic —but concentrated—is not pure orange juice. • Might position it against Britvic rather than Club.
Kisqua	• Pronunciation initially difficult, but quickly overcome. • Very definite and individualistic name. • Novel and unique brand name. • Drew favourable emotional relationships. • International and cosmopolitan—potential to be a 'world brand'. • Elegant and sophisticated. • High quality and accessible.	• The best representative of the new product. • Much more depth than other concept alternatives. • Good impact, will generate trial easily. • Stylish yet solidly in the mainstream of soft drinks—but a bit too straightforward? • Very good typography.

Ballygowan believed that by working on Kisqua's colour and sweetness they could significantly improve its appeal to the market, and also develop much higher ratings by fine-tuning Kisqua's advertising strategy. Response to Kisqua's name was positive: 71 per cent liked the name Kisqua compared to 20 per cent who did not. When assessing Kisqua's label, 36 per cent of respondents considered it above average, 36 per cent average and 26 per cent below average.

Two advertising concepts were presented. 'Kisqua—what could be more natural' received better than average scores from 38 per cent of respondents, while 45 per cent rated it average. Projective tests associated Kisqua with sports-minded and health-conscious people and with people who really care about quality and who may be described as trendsetters. The target market was confirmed as soft-drink consumers in social classes ABC1C2, 15-30 years, and of either sex. Following the research, Dimension made the appropriate adjustment to the advertising concept.

Pack design was a very important aspect of this project. Ballygowan had proprietorial rights to their distinctive bottle designs used for their spring water range. However, they believed that Kisqua should be differentiated from their other products and that the branding and bottle design of Kisqua should help distinguish it within the soft-drinks market. The pack design assumed that Kisqua would compete directly with Club Orange.

Business Plan

Initially the business plan had Kisqua available in three pack sizes: 1.5 litre plastic, 250 ml. glass and 330 ml. cans. Distribution would be through the existing Ballygowan network of grocery, wholesalers (grocery and bottlers), cash-and-carry and independent outlets.

Three pricing options were considered: a low pricing strategy which would put Kisqua into the market with prices comparable to Coke and 7-Up, a medium pricing strategy, and a high pricing strategy positioning Kisqua as a premium brand. Early projections gave strategies yielding the following percentage market shares in 1990:

	Plastic	Cans	Overall
Low-price strategy	4.2	3.1	3.0
Medium-price strategy	3.3	2.2	2.1
High-price strategy	2.1	1.5	1.6

1. Includes plastic bottles, cans and glass bottles.

The Marketing Department projected that these volumes would increase by 33 per cent during the second year and by 16 per cent during the third year. After three years and assuming a medium pricing stategy, Kisqua's market share would be approximately 3 per cent of Ireland's soft-drinks market. This compared with Club Orange's 10 per cent market share in 1990.

With a capital investment of 1£1.5 million and 1£120,000 for additional technical staff, generous trade margins and all other relevant costs, the profits projections before tax for Kisqua were as set out in Exhibit 6.10.

The medium pricing strategy aimed at a retail selling price of 1£1.19 per 1.5 litre bottle and 40 p per can in supermarkets. This gave a reasonable return on investment and room to discount to supermarkets to compete with Coke and 7-Up if necessary (see Exhibit 6.11).

EXHIBIT 6.10	Profit projection before tax for Kisqua (1£'000)		
	Year 1	**Year 2**	**Year 3**
Low price strategy			
Low volume	(311)	(129)	(36)
Likely volume	(33)	241	382
High volume	262	634	825
Medium price strategy			
Low volume	(371)	(211)	(128)
Likely volume	(63)	200	336
High volume	341	702	902
High price strategy			
Low volume	(346)	(177)	90
Likely volume	(84)	172	304
High volume	297	690	876

Test Market

From August to October 1990 Ballygowan test marketed Kisqua as a pasteurized drink in 250 ml. glass bottles. The test was conducted in the Dublin area using Ballygowan's main independent distributor serving 250 CTNs (combined confectioner, tobacconist and newsagent's), delicatessens and petrol stations. The results were discouraging. Most of the negative reaction centred around the pack and retailers not knowing where to position the range in their store. Ballygowan now faced a difficult decision. Should they withdraw Kisqua altogether, redesign and reposition it, or go ahead as originally planned? They knew that if they were to delay and relaunch, the payback of the expensive research and development would be put back considerably.

EXHIBIT 6.11	Kisqua: business plan for year 1		
	1.5L Pet	**250 ml. bottles**	**330 ml. cans**
Retail selling price (1£)	1.05	—	0.33
Net revenue per case wholesale (1£)	8.44	7.00	5.30
Volume (cases)			
low	200,000	30,000	125,000
likely	300,000	50,000	175,000
high	400,000	75,000	225,000
Retail selling price (1£)	1.19	—	0.40
Net revenue per case wholesale (1£)	8.93	7.00	6.00

Volume (cases)			
low	125,000	30,000	75,000
likely	200,000	50,000	125,000
high	300,000	75,000	175,000
Retail selling price (1£)	1.29	—	0.45
Net revenue per case wholesale (1£)	9.68	7.00	6.50
Volume (cases)			
low	100,000	30,000	60,000
likely	150,000	50,000	85,000
high	225,000	75,000	125,000

Questions

1. Examine the types of market research used by Ballygowan in the development of Kisqua. What sort of information were they hoping to get from the different methods they used? Is quantitative marketing research intrinsically more reliable then qualitative research?
2. Relate the market research to the stages in the product development process and explain their use. Were the methods appropriately used? What alternatives would you suggest? How did they contribute to Ballygowan's understanding of the strategy for launching Kisqua?
3. Why could in-depth marketing research lead to wrong strategic choices? Do marketing research errors explain Kisqua's poor test market showing? What does explain the poor showing? Was too much, or too little, market research done by Ballygowan?
4. Where should Ballygowan go from here? What extra research should they do, if any? Should they go ahead with the existing marketing strategy, reposition the product, start again or give in?

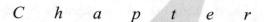

TELUS
PLAnet

IVEY

Krista K. Wylie prepared this case under the supervision of Elizabeth M.A. Grasby, Pre-Business Program Director, solely to provide material for class discussion. The authors do not intend to illustrate either effective or ineffective handling of a managerial situation. The authors may have disguised certain names and other identifying information to protect confidentiality.

It was July 1, 1995, as Gemini Waghmare, the product manager for TELUS' PLAnet Internet Access Service, and Myron Borys, the general manager of Internet at TELUS, were putting together their business plan to bring the large telecommunication firm's newest product to market. With the launch date for PLAnet set for August 1995, Gemini and Myron knew they must quickly complete their marketing plan for the Alberta-based corporation.

TELUS

TELUS Corporation was a relatively new company whose largest subsidiaries, TELUS Communications (formerly Alberta Government Telephone) and TELUS Communications

Edmonton (formerly ED TEL), had been the sole telephone companies for the province of Alberta, Canada, for over 100 years. The two major TELUS operating companies combined to provide telephone services to every household and business in Alberta and had total revenues of over $2 billion annually. Alberta, which was one of Canada's western provinces, had a population of approximately 2.5 million people as of 1991. The principal industries in this province were chemical products, mining, agriculture, food, manufacturing, construction, and oil production and refinement.

Given its long history in the province, TELUS developed a reputation as the dependable, reliable provider of communications services for Albertans. The company prided itself on enhancing the lives of its customers through telecommunications and enjoyed being known as a solid company servicing its clients needs well... After all, what was more reliable than the dial tone?

After several years of long distance market share erosion, the TELUS corporation's strategic plans for the future included strong growth through aggressive market strategies and a renewed focus on the customer and service. Launching an Internet service was one part of this strategy. The name PLAnet was chosen, with the first three letters intentionally capitalized to form the acronym Public Live Access network.

INTERNET SERVICE PROVIDERS

By the mid-1990s, the worldwide "network of networks" referred to as the Internet was recognized as a means to communicate with people all over the world, at a fraction of the cost of long distance calls. The World Wide Web, the first multimedia forum for the Internet, offered entertainment, shopping, information and educational content to a mass market. By late 1994, it was believed the Internet had attracted over 25 million users and this figure was estimated to hit 100 million by the end of 1997.[1]

An Internet Service Provider (ISP) was any firm that offered access to the Internet. Setting up business as an ISP was easy and could be done virtually anywhere, provided that a communications link to the Internet could be rented and that telephone lines could be leased from the local phone company (see Exhibit 1). Once the telephone lines, which formed the "network architecture," were in place, hardware components called routers directed the flow of Internet traffic. The necessary infrastructure components also included modems, which allowed clients to connect to the ISP, and servers, which stored ISP specific data such as news, mail and administrative information.

ISPs could provide "dial-up" services or "dedicated" Internet service. "Dial-up" services were typically used by households and small businesses, which used a modem and a personal computer to dial into their ISP in order to retrieve mail or surf[2] the World Wide Web. Dial-up connections ranged in price from $9.95 to $49.95 per month, depending upon the hours of usage offered and the software and services provided. "Dedicated" connections were almost exclusively used by large corporations which shared a permanent Internet connection with their employees over a networked system. A dedicated connection ranged in price from $400 to $2,000 per month.

By the summer of 1995, over 50 ISPs existed in the province of Alberta. It was anticipated that the demand for these ISPs would continue. This growth was of concern to telephone com-

---

1. http://www.anamorph.com
2. "Surfing" was the popular term for randomly exploring content of the World Wide Web.

panies because ISPs leased network services only to use them for services that cannibalized a telephone company's long distance revenues. Long distance business had, for years, been a profitable area of a telephone company's operations. Given the threat of ISPs on revenues, most telephone companies in North America in 1995 had plans underway to launch an Internet service.

The Market

It was estimated that out of the approximately one million households TELUS served, 45 per cent owned personal computers (PCs) in 1994 and 40 per cent of these PC owners also owned modems, which were necessary to access the Internet. Myron and Gemini expected growth of 10-15 percentage points per year in both PC and modem ownership for the next five years. As well, there were approximately 50,000 small businesses in Alberta that could be served by the dial-up Internet Service TELUS wanted to provide. Of these businesses, Myron and Gemini estimated that 80 per cent of them owned PCs but that only 55 per cent of these PC-equipped businesses owned modems. They anticipated that by 1999, 95 per cent of small businesses would own PCs and 70 per cent of these businesses would own modems.

Four Consumer Profiles

Four consumer profiles had been identified by TELUS: Professionals, Internet Junkies, Internet Graduates, and General Majority Internet Neophytes. The specific benefits sought by each consumer group varied significantly and had been identified by Myron and Gemini (see Exhibit 2).

Professionals

The professionals were individuals who accessed the Internet either through a dial-up access from their home or small business or through a business dedicated Internet connection. They usually required some training, were less price-sensitive than other consumers and had little time to dedicate to the Internet. Professionals constituted approximately 25 per cent of the market who accessed the Internet at home and virtually 100 per cent of the market who accessed the Internet at work.

Internet Junkies

Internet Junkies were, on average, males between 21–30 years of age with some form of post-secondary education. They spent 25 to 40 hours per week on the Internet, primarily browsing and posting their own content on the World Wide Web, and almost always accessed the Internet from home. This group represented a large portion of Internet users, but their share of total usage was decreasing due to the growing adoption of the Internet by the mainstream population.

Internet Graduates

Internet Graduates were identified as a hybrid between the Internet Professional and the Internet Junkie. Members of this group were between 21–30 years of age and had been educated within an atmosphere where Internet was taught, or offered free of charge. Having entered the working world, these people sought a commercial Internet Access provider, required no training on the Internet and were slightly price-sensitive. The Internet Junkies and Internet Graduates combined represented approximately 25 per cent of the market.

General Majority Internet Neophytes

The General Majority Internet Neophytes were individuals attracted to the Internet who were interested in exploring and becoming familiar with the highly touted technology. They represented the mass market and had limited knowledge of the Internet's capabilities and how to use it with their home computer. These consumers purchased Internet services for various reasons, including wanting knowledge for themselves or their children, satisfying a curiosity about the technology or "because everyone else has it". They viewed having the Internet in the home as a luxury and, as such, were somewhat price-conscious.

Competition

In 1995, there were over 50 small ISPs in Alberta that operated in homes, small office spaces, or in the back room of computer stores. These ISPs had and continued to enjoy the quick growth in their business; however, their lack of time, talent and financial resources often meant that, although their prices were low, their service to their customers was poor. For instance, many of the smaller ISPs did not have a sufficient number of modems, resulting in long wait times and busy signals for their subscribers. Others did not have enough server space and subscribers were, therefore, unable to access everything the Internet had to offer. For example, an ISP with inadequate server space could only provide a limited number of newsgroups[3] to its subscribers. Most importantly, the networks used by these firms were often unreliable, with no back-up lines in place; therefore, if a main line was out of service, subscribers had no access to Internet service until the problem had been corrected.

A few proprietary on-line services such as Compuserve and America Online were also available to Albertan residents. These proprietary on-line services offered access to both the Internet and pay-per-use discussion forums and interest groups. A proprietary on-line service was different than other ISPs because it offered on-line content that was only made available to subscribers of the service. These content offerings provided much more variety to users and allowed these companies to charge premiums for connection times for these on-line services.

By late 1994, information had been compiled on a sample of ISPs (Exhibit 3 and Exhibit 4). Gemini knew this information would be helpful in determining what, specifically, TELUS should offer its Internet subscribers and what an appropriate pricing strategy for PLAnet might be. TELUS could offer low-service packages at low prices with the risk of compromising reliability and service or it could offer high-service packages at the risk of pricing itself out of the market.

Corporate Capabilities

TELUS wanted to continue as the primary communications provider in Alberta and, thus, was interested in playing a large role in Internet services. Currently, the information technol-

---

3. A newsgroup was a text-only collection of articles that relate to a specific topic.

ogy, customer service and network engineering departments of TELUS were being used by PLAnet but as the Internet service grew, PLAnet would need its own infrastructure of dedicated resources so that it could "stand alone." TELUS was optimistic that the Internet could become a profitable business. There were champions of the service on the Executive team who were willing to commit any resources required to ensure the success of PLAnet.

DECISIONS TO BE MADE

Organizational Structure

TELUS was the telephone company that provided local service and, as such, was a monopoly service provider in Alberta. As a result, TELUS was subject to regulation by the Canadian Radio-television Telecommunications Commission (CRTC). The CRTC was a government-administered regulatory body that ensured monopoly businesses within the telecommunications industry acted in a fair manner to their consumer base and within the local business arena. If PLAnet were kept under the auspices of TELUS, TELUS would have to file a tariff with the CRTC and receive regulatory approval before launching the service. This was a risky and cumbersome option for a number of reasons. Firstly, the CRTC could rule that TELUS be disallowed from competing in the ISP market due to a potential conflict of interest since the telephone company would be entering a competitive business using the same telephone lines for which it held a monopoly. Secondly, even with CRTC approval, TELUS PLAnet would then be committed, as a regulated entity, to seek approval from the CRTC for every service amendment and price change the company wanted to make. Thirdly, because the CRTC evaluation and approval process often took months and involved a public notification process, all of PLAnet's competitors would have the benefit of knowing TELUS' strategic plans before they were implemented.

Alternately, TELUS could remove PLAnet from the CRTC regulated company and operate it under a non-regulated subsidiary. Without regulation, PLAnet would not have to report its cost structures, revenue projections and business plans to the CRTC. However, if PLAnet were to be separate from TELUS, PLAnet would be unable to install hardware on TELUS premises, to include PLAnet charges on the TELUS local phone bill, or to capitalize on any economies of scale that might be gained by operating PLAnet under TELUS. These major cost implications would have to be weighed carefully against the benefits of operating a business free from regulation in such a dynamic industry.

Once a decision had been made about whether or not PLAnet should operate separately from TELUS, Gemini and Myron could develop the actual marketing strategy for PLAnet.

Promotion

The decision had been made to sell the Internet service via a 1-800 number and in selected Phone Centres throughout Alberta. Firm decisions had yet to be made regarding advertising. Consideration was being given to mainstream media such as newspapers and radio, and to inserts within TELUS phone bills and niche advertising such as ads in computer papers. An Alberta-wide campaign using any combination of the above-mentioned media was estimated to cost $75,000/week to reach effective coverage. Outdoor billboards would cost approximately $300/month. Gemini and Myron had decided that television advertising focused solely on PLAnet would be too expensive to justify; however, they might be able to integrate

PLAnet into other TELUS advertisements. Obviously, if TELUS was run as a separate entity, joint television ads and TELUS bill inserts would not be possible. Another promotional method being considered was the use of giveaways as a sign-up reward. PLAnet mousepads, clocks, pins and calling cards could be used at a cost of $6.00, $8.00, $1.00 and $5.00, respectively.

Final Considerations

TELUS needed to determine the ratio of subscribers to modems. Providing one modem for every 15 subscribers would ensure top quality service, but they could have as many as 30 subscribers per modem. TELUS' cost for one modem would be $700, which would not include the $1000 per year cost per modem for maintaining the lines for each modem. Other costs to be considered are given in Exhibit 5.

In addition to the costs associated with each subscriber, TELUS would have to spend close to $6 million in start-up costs for things such as servers, routers, terminal services, work stations for help-desk employees, and new billing and tracking systems. These start-up costs could reasonably be allocated over three years. Other annual expenses were estimated at $500,000 for maintenance, $7,500,000 for fixed labor, and $550,000 for other related expenses. Advertising costs would depend on the promotional strategy chosen.

As Myron and Gemini considered all the information before them, they knew they had many decisions to make before the launch of TELUS PLAnet.

EXHIBIT 1 **Internet Service Provider Technical Infrastructure Overview**

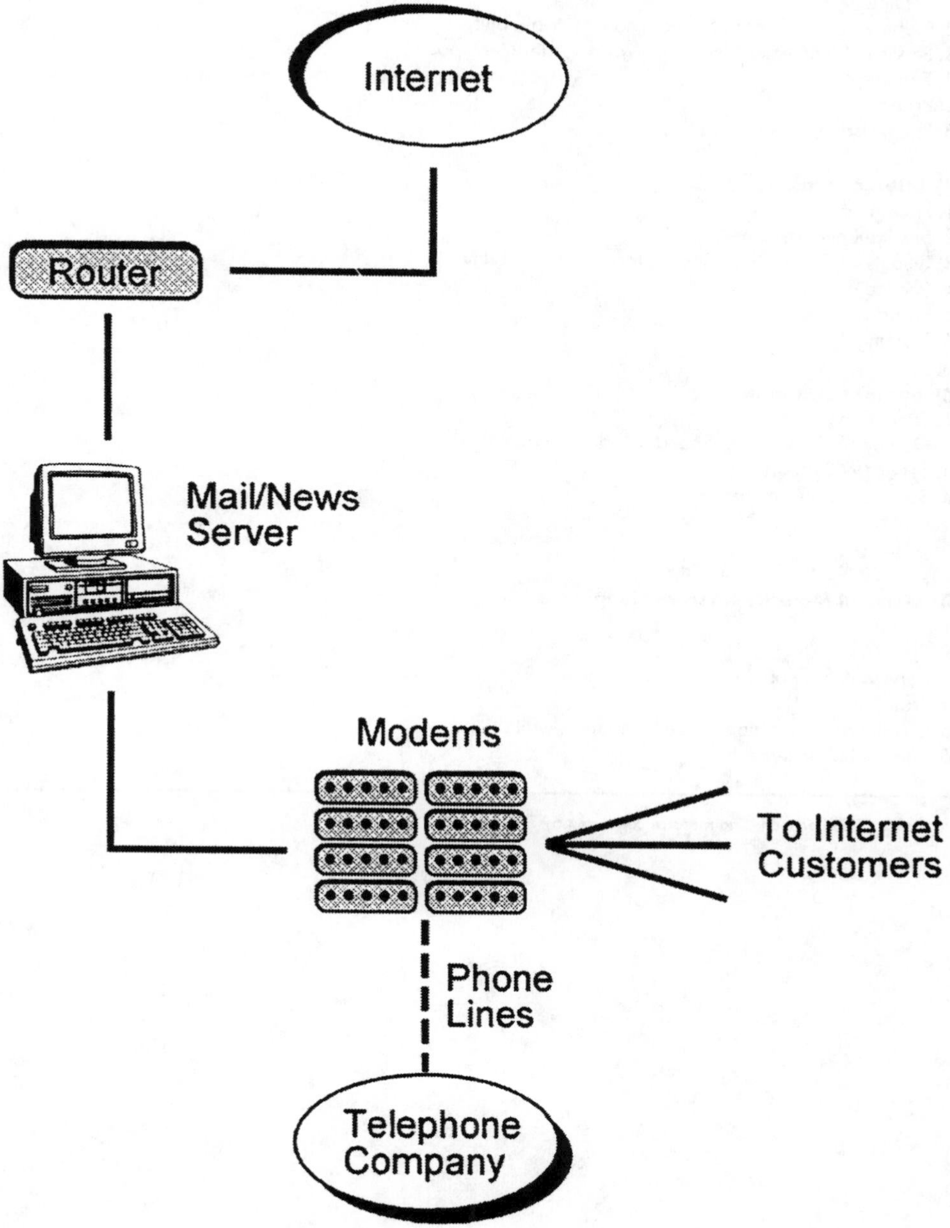

Internet

Router

Mail/News
Server

Modems

To Internet
Customers

Phone
Lines

Telephone
Company

| **EXHIBIT 2** | **Benefits Sought by Each Consumer Segment[4]** |

A) Professional
1. Service & Support
2. Quality of Connection, Speed, Modem Availability
3. Service Enhancements such as World Wide Web space
4. Training
5. Brand
6. Price/Usage

B) Internet Junkie
1. Price/Usage
2. Service Enhancements
3. Quality of Connection, Speed, Modem Availability
4. Service & Support
5. Brand
6. Training

C) Internet Graduate
1. Price/Usage
2. Quality of Connection, Speed, Modem Availability
3. Service & Support
4. Service Enhancements
5. Brand
6. Training

D) General Majority Internet Neophytes
1. Brand
2. Price/Usage
3. Service & Support
4. Training
5. Quality of Connection, Speed, Modem Availability
6. Service Enhancements

4. Source: Based on marketing research conducted by *TELUS*.

EXHIBIT 3   Comparison of ISPs[5]

Service Provider	Modem Pool[6]	Setup Fee	Monthly Package Rate	Hourly Rate Afterwards	Helpdesk Services	Software Provided
Alberta SuperNET	28	$30.00	$30.00 for 40 hours	$2.00/hour	2 people	Full complement
CCNet	32	$55.00 with book	$35.00 for 35 hours	$1.00/hour	24-hour service	Full complement
Compu Serve	Unknown	$25.00 starter kit	$34.00 for 20 hours	$2.75/hour	Extended hours	Proprietary software
Compu Smart	16	None	$30.00 for 40 hours	$1.50/hour	Normal office hours	Partial complement
OANet	10	$29.95	$19.95 for 25 hours	$2.00/hour	Normal office hours	Partial complement
TicNet	8	$40.00	$30.00 for 20 hours	$2.00/hour	Normal office hours	Partial complement

5. Source: Based on marketing research conducted by *TELUS*.
6. Number of customers per modem.

EXHIBIT 4   Costs for Various Levels of Usage

Service Provider	Cost per month based on typical usage	Cost per month based on 50 hours	Cost per month based on 100 hours
Alberta SuperNET	$30.00	$50.00	$150.00
CCNet	$30.00	$50.00	$100.00
CompuServe	$61.50	$116.50	$254.00
CompuSmart	$30.00	$45.00	$120.00
OANet	$29.95	$69.95	$170.00
TicNet	$50.00	$90.00	$190.00

*Typical usage is 30 hours per month.

EXHIBIT 5   TELUS' Costs Per Subscriber

One-time Labor Cost for Set-up	$20.00/customer
Helpdesk cost	$40.00/customer/year for high quality $20.00/customer/year for lower quality
Software kit one-time cost	$20.00/customer for high quality $10.00/customer for lower quality
Hardware systems	$80.00/customer/year

Chapter 5

SKYWARD AVIATION– ROUTE EXPANSION

IVEY

On Monday, June 6, 1995, Frank Behrendt, president of Skyward Aviation (Skyward), laid out the task for J.M. Smith, manager of business and corporate development:

> Calm Air is making a lot of money and Canadian North may be pulling jet service out of Thompson. Business travellers are sick and tired of getting up really early to catch a 7:00 a.m. flight out of Winnipeg to Thompson. Consumers are also tired of paying exorbitant fares. I think we should offer scheduled service into Winnipeg and other communities in Manitoba. I want you to see if this will work and present your findings and a marketing plan at the July 15 Board of Directors' meeting.

Skyward Aviation was a regional aviation company providing scheduled, charter and aeromedical service. Skyward was based in Thompson, Manitoba, Canada, with additional aircraft and offices in Winnipeg, Manitoba; Norway House, Manitoba; and Rankin Inlet, Northwest Territories.

COMPANY HISTORY

Thompson, Manitoba, was a city of 22,000 people, located in central northern Manitoba and known as "the Hub of the North". The main industries of Thompson included a large nickel mine (International Nickel Company, Inco), transportation and government.

Skyward was founded January 2, 1987, when three partners purchased a small local air service that was almost bankrupt. Skyward began with five aircraft, a hangar, a small office building and fifteen employees. Frank Behrendt, one of the partners and a pilot in northern Canada for a number of years, was appointed president. Prior to the purchase, the company provided an air charter service for passengers, carried freight and performed the occasional medical evacuation from outlying communities around Thompson.

Because of the company's poor reputation, the new partners wanted to deal with some of the obvious weaknesses of its operations. Customers had been unhappy with the level of service, the aircraft were aging, and the aircraft came from three different manufacturers. This had resulted in plummeting revenue, high maintenance costs and high inventory carrying loss. The partners immediately began a fleet renewal process, expanding the fleet with fewer aircraft from one manufacturer.

SCHEDULED SERVICE

After seeing a significant turnaround in customers' acceptance of the company, management decided to provide scheduled service to a number of communities where they had previously done a high volume of charter work. Scheduled service differed from charter service, in that a scheduled flight left a specific community on a pre-determined date and time and customers reserved seats on the aircraft. Charter service required customers to reserve an aircraft for their specific use. From a business perspective, scheduled service had more risk since revenue was not guaranteed for all seats on the aircraft. Skyward began scheduled service on September 1, 1988, from Thompson (Manitoba) to York Landing (Manitoba) and to Gods River (Manitoba).

Currently, Skyward served fifteen communities in northern Manitoba and the Northwest Territories (see Exhibit 1 for the company's brochure and the system schedule for Manitoba). With the introduction of new communities, Skyward used an entry pricing strategy of 30 to 40 percent below the competition. Skyward management rationalized that prices were very high due to a lack of competition and Skyward wanted to give consumers a break. The competition responded and closed the price gap very quickly but Skyward was able to pick up a small market share.

In the spring of 1994, Skyward purchased two Embrear Banditerantes (Bandits), 15-seat aircraft. A Bandit had short takeoff and landing characteristics with a high useable weight for an aircraft in its class, ideal for the conditions in northern Manitoba. Each Bandit had a large cargo door in the back and was sent out in a configuration utilizing both freight and passengers. The freight was sent on standby so that the airplane usually realized very high load factors because the freight 'topped off' the aircraft. Freight generated less revenue than passengers, but Skyward could guarantee next-day delivery into remote communities because of its daily service and could, therefore, charge a much higher per pound rate than its competitors.

It was at this time that Skyward began to focus on increasing the number of passengers and revenue per flight (yield management). By the summer of 1994, Skyward had a significant market share of scheduled traffic in and out of northern Manitoba communities and had done this with no formal advertising.

In early 1995, Skyward purchased two more Bandits. The purchase of these last two aircraft complemented the first two, because all routes could be served by Bandits. This helped enhance passenger appeal, and by June 1995, passengers carried were on target for 25 percent growth over the 1994 level of 35,000.

Skyward's growth in the scheduled service market was also attributed to aircraft flexibility and exceptional customer service. Skyward was currently operating seven types of aircraft, sixteen aircraft in total. Because of the different types of aircraft, smaller aircraft could be substituted and costs reduced if passenger and cargo loads were down on certain days.

The customer base in and out of Thompson was small and 90 percent of business was repeat customers. The employees and management of Skyward were committed to serving the customer and customers often returned to Skyward in response to that commitment. Skyward was the first carrier in Thompson to provide food on flights, offer free shuttle service into town from the airport and run errands for out-of-town customers at no charge.

Skyward's existing reservation system was very inefficient and much of the work was done manually. Skyward required all reservations and all data processing to go through head office. If a travel agent wanted to book a passenger on a flight from Thompson to Shammattawa, the travel agent had to call Thompson and ask a Skyward agent to check availability and make the reservation. The system also did not provide the necessary marketing information for management to make effective and timely decisions.

THE MANITOBA MARKET

Over the years, Frank Behrendt had toyed with the idea of providing scheduled service to Winnipeg from Thompson, but as other opportunities had presented themselves, resources were directed to those opportunities.

Scheduled air transportation in Manitoba was currently served by four main regional carriers: Canadian North Airlines, Calm Air Ltd., Perimeter Airlines and Skyward Aviation. There were also a number of other carriers which provided scheduled service to a few communities.

Canadian North Airlines, based in Edmonton, Alberta, was a division of Canadian Airlines that provided Boeing 737 jet service (125 passengers) to a number of communities in northern Canada (Alberta, Manitoba, Northwest Territories, Quebec) (see Exhibit 2 for Canadian North system schedule for Manitoba). Because of Canadian Airline's cash flow problems, Canadian Airlines was continually reviewing operations and restructuring to cut marginal services and reduce expenses. Routes were being turned over to regional connectors to be served with smaller turboprop aircraft. It was believed that, within the year, the routes in Manitoba would no longer be served by Boeing 737 service.

Calm Air, based in Thompson, Manitoba, was a Canadian Airlines Connector (45% ownership by Canadian Airlines) and was the largest passenger carrier in Manitoba (see Exhibit 3 for Calm Air system schedule for selected routes in Manitoba). Calm Air had had very limited competition for almost 20 years and the owners enjoyed a healthy financial position.

Perimeter Airlines served communities in southern Manitoba out of its Winnipeg base operation which was similar to Skyward Aviation. Perimeter Airlines operated 15 - 19 passenger aircraft and moved approximately 20,000 more passengers than Skyward.

Air transportation customers in the north could be divided into two groups: business and leisure customers. Business travellers made up 65 to 75 percent of passengers on the considered routes. Most passengers (70 percent) travelling from Winnipeg to Thompson flew the direct flight in the morning and evening. More information needed to be gathered but it was known that passengers considered price, departure times, on-time departure, flight time, connections, food and other amenities, aircraft (size, cleanliness, appearance), employee courteousness, baggage handling and extra baggage charges as important factors in their decision. Leisure travellers usually made travel plans well in advance of flight date.

RECENT DEVELOPMENTS

In February 1995, Calm Air replaced its aging Hawker Siddely 748 (48-passenger prop aerocraft) aircraft with brand new SAAB 340B Plus (30-passenger turboprop aircraft, which were fast and comfortable) aircraft. Three more SAAB 340B Plus's were on order along with one SAAB 2000 (50-seat turboprop aircraft, the fastest turboprop on the market). With the new aircraft, Calm Air offered direct flights from Winnipeg (Manitoba) to Thompson (Manitoba), Flin Flon (Manitoba), and The Pas (Manitoba), complementing Canadian North's service. It was estimated by Skyward's management that Calm Air would realize a profit of $750,000/year on the SAAB 340. Calm Air's new afternoon flights from Thompson to Winnipeg had been successful and the Thursday and Friday flights were always full. Exhibit 4 shows the mileage between selected communities in Manitoba and the Northwest Territories. Fares and passenger loads for Calm Air and Canadian North are shown in Exhibit 5.

Calm Air was involved heavily in the community-supporting races, radio programs and other community events. Calm Air heavily promoted the new direct service with the SAAB 340B Plus aircraft. Calm Air used the reservation system of its parent, Canadian Airline, and American Airlines (Sabre system). This system had features such as interactive display and sell which allowed travel agents to inquire and make reservations without the requirement of personal contact with Calm Air.

The federal government, currently run by the Liberal party, as part one of its promises to aboriginal peoples of Canada in the 1994 election 'Red Book', was proposing the Strategic Procurement Initiative (SPI). SPI stated that "the program is intended to apply to all procurement (purchases) by all federal government departments and agencies …as long as there is at least one qualified and available aboriginal supplier (50%-owned by aboriginal individuals), no further competition would be sought".[1] Skyward's owners were not aboriginal people. Forty percent of Skyward's current revenue was from direct federal government purchases.

EXPANDED ROUTE CONSIDERATIONS

There were a number of options to consider before making a decision to proceed with the expanded route structure.

Aircraft Decision

One alternative, which would require only minimal adjustment to existing operations, would be to use one of the Embrear Banditerantes on the Thompson to Winnipeg route. Prior to launching this service, the aircraft would need a new interior at a cost of $10,000. This renovation could be completed in one month.

---

1. Public Works and Government Services document (Briefing SPI, January 1995, pp. 10, 11).

Another alternative would entail Skyward purchasing a new aircraft. Manufacturers required a lead time of four to six months for delivery of aircraft. Exhibit 6 lists cost and performance information for four appropriate turboprop aircraft, as well as Calm Air's SAAB 340B Plus and the Embrear Banditerante. With a new aircraft purchase, a number of variables would have to be considered: cost, performance, payload , and the ease with which a new aircraft could fit into existing operations.

Other Costs

A number of things would happen once a decision was made to purchase a new aircraft.

Approval from the National Transportation Agency for a 'transport' category aircraft (greater than 12,500 lbs) would be needed since the aircraft would be larger than any of Skyward's existing aircraft. Second, certain operations procedures would need to be rewritten because different regulations applied. This would also require revisions to the operations manual.

Third, the maintenance department would need to hire engineers with qualifications to maintain this type of airplane as well as purchase specialized maintenance equipment at a cost of $50,000 to $75,000. For each of the new communities Skyward would serve, Winnipeg being the exception, the company would need to invest $25,000 in ground support equipment such as ground power units, de-icing equipment and boarding/deboarding aids.

Fourth, the flight department would need to recruit and/or train pilots that would have the qualifications to fly the new aircraft. If one aircraft was purchased, five pilots and three flight attendants would need to be recruited and trained. If two aircraft were purchased, eight pilots and six flight attendants would need to be recruited and trained. Training contracts would need to be negotiated with training schools in the United States. A three-week program would cost $25,000 per crew member. The average salary with benefits for a pilot would be $52,150 and for a flight attendant would be $22,000.

With new scheduled service, the following other costs would be incurred: landing and terminal fees at all airports would be $50 per flight; food for passengers could be contracted out at $5.00 per passenger; newspapers and magazines would cost $1.00 per passenger. In Winnipeg, passenger check-in, boarding and baggage handling could be contracted from Air Canada for $120 per flight. Terminal operations in Thompson (rental, computer, communications, supplies, etc) would cost approximately $75,000 annually, if boarding was moved from Skyward's building to the main terminal. Terminal operations in other communities would be approximately $35,000 annually.

Automating The Reservation System

Skyward was considering upgrading and automating the reservation system. Skyward had contacted Advantis Canada Ltd. to provide automation service. Advantis provided distribution (via computer) of an airline's flight schedules, gave fare information to travel agencies through the Galileo network and managed inventory (seats). The system allowed travel agents to enquire about specific seats on flights, reserve those seats and take payment from customers. With Advantis, collection of fares was done through a central banking group. Travel agents took an eight and one half percent commission for a sale. To contract Advantis costs would include a $50,000 initial one-time setup cost and communication, hardware and miscellaneous costs of $25,000 per year, $1.20 per passenger for all passengers booked (by Skyward agent or travel agent) and an additional $1.20 per passenger for passengers booked on Galileo system (travel agent). Advantis required a lead time of five months to implement the system.

The Manager of Business and Corporate Development began to review the above information to evaluate its feasibility and the time needed before beginning this new scheduled service. Skyward Aviation was a profitable company, but the size of the expansion and investment would require the majority of financing to be debt-financed. He had decisions to make about what communities to serve, the schedule, design and the pricing and promotional strategy to be implemented (Exhibit 7 gives cost information). The average North American airline spent three percent of revenue on advertising on established routes.

EXHIBIT 1   Company Brochure and System Schedule for Manitoba

CHARTER SERVICES:

Whether you want a fifteen minute skytour, a week long sales trip through the arctic, or to move a ton of freight, Skyward's charter services face the challenge of meeting Northern Manitoba's varied transportation needs, from freight delivery to executive transport. Skyward Aviation is there for you:

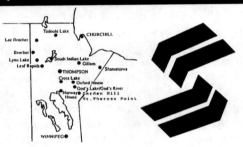

- Freight forwarding
- Group charters
- Fly out fishing
- Emergency services

SKYWARD AVIATION
SERVING NORTHERN MANITOBA
778-7088
or
1-800-665-0638

SKYCARE SERVICES:

At Skyward we know the importance of professional Medevac service. Our specially trained crews, stationed in Thompson and Norway House, and our **Citation Jet** and **Cessna 421** are dedicated to provide this emergency service to the North. SkyCare is privileged to assist Northern Manitoba's health care agencies by providing a vital link to remote communities. SkyCare offers:

- Dedicated aircraft
- Specialized equipment
- 24 hour availability
- Aeromedically trained flight nurses & crew

For more information on our services in Manitoba or the Keewatin district call our offices in:

Rankin Inlet
PH: 819-645-3200
FAX: 819-645-3208

Winnipeg
PH: 204-888-8664
FAX: 204-888-8665

Norway House
PH: 204-359-4900

SCHEDULE SERVICES:

DEPART FROM		ARRIVING IN		FREQUENCY
Thompson	08:30	Oxford House	09:20	Mon – Sat
Oxford House	09:40	Thompson	10:20	
Thompson	14:00	Oxford House	14:50	Mon – Sat
Oxford House	15:10	Thompson	16:00	
Thompson	10:00	York Landing	10:30	Mon – Sat
York Landing	10:50	Thompson	11:20	
Thompson	17:15	York Landing	17:45	Fri & Sat
York Landing	18:00	Thompson	18:30	
Thompson	09:00	Lac Brochet	10:20	
Lac Brochet	10:40	Brochet	11:00	Mon,Wed,Fri
Brochet	11:15	Thompson	12:25	
Thompson	09:00	Lynn Lake	09:55	
Lynn Lake	10:15	Brochet	10:50	Tues & Thurs
Brochet	11:05	Lac Brochet	11:25	
Lac Brochet	11:45	Lynn Lake	12:30	
Lynn Lake	12:50	Thompson	13:45	
Thompson	13:00	Lac Brochet	14:20	
Lac Brochet	14:40	Brochet	15:00	Sat
Brochet	15:20	Thompson	16:30	
Thompson	10:45	Tadoule	12:05	Mon – Sat
Tadoule	12:25	Thompson	12:35	

SPRING 95

DEPART FROM		ARRIVING IN		FREQUENCY
Thompson	12:00	Gods Narrows	13:00	
Gods Narrows	13:20	Gods River	13:45	Tues, Thurs
Gods River	14:00	Thompson	15:00	& Sat
Thompson	12:00	Gods River	13:00	
Gods River	13:20	Gods Narrows	13:45	Mon, Wed, Fri
Gods Narrows	14:00	Thompson	15:00	
Thompson	13:00	Garden Hill	14:10	
Garden Hill	14:30	St. Theresa	14:45	Mon, Wed, Fri
St.Theresa	15:00	Thompson	16:10	
Thompson	15:30	Shamattawa	16:45	Tues, Thurs,
Shamattawa	17:05	Thompson	18:20	& Sat
Thompson	15:30	Shamattawa	16:45	Mon, Wed, Fri
Shamattawa	17:05	Gillam	17:50	
Gillam	18:10	Thompson	19:05	
Thompson	16:30	South Indian	17:05	Mon – Sat
South Indian	17:25	Thompson	18:00	

Check-in: 30 min. prior to flight.
Skyward provides complimentary lunches on all flights over 1 hour.
Baggage allowance: 70 lbs per ticket.
Skyward has complimentary shuttle service from your flight into Thompson.

EXHIBIT 2	Canadian Airlines North—Manitoba		
Date of the Week	**Origin**	**Destination**	**Times**
12345	Winnipeg	Thompson	07:00 - 08:15
12345	Thompson	Flin Flon	08:40 - 09:20
12345	Flin Flon	Winnipeg	09:40 - 10:40
135	Winnipeg	Gillam	11:20 - 12:40
135	Gillam	Churchill	13:05 - 13:45
135	Churchill	Winnipeg	14:15 - 16:25
123457	Winnipeg	The Pas	17:55 - 19:00
123457	The Pas	Thompson	19:25 - 20:05
123457	Thompson	Winnipeg	20:35 - 21:40

EXHIBIT 3	Calm Air System Schedule—Selected Routes in Manitoba		
Date of the Week	**Origin**	**Destination**	**Times**
123456	Winnipeg	The Pas	07:30 - 08:59
12345	The Pas	Winnipeg	09:25 - 10:34
6	The Pas	Flin Flon	09:25 - 09:46
6	Flin Flon	Winnipeg	10:05 - 11:25
12345	Winnipeg	Thompson	14:20 - 16:05
12345	Thompson	Winnipeg	16:35 - 18:00
6	Thompson	Winnipeg	08:40 - 10:24
6	Winnipeg	Thompson	12:00 - 13:45
7	Winnipeg	Thompson	14:20 - 16:17
7	Thompson	Winnipeg	16:35 - 18:00
12357	Winnipeg	Flin Flon	18:30 - 20:00
12357	Flin Flon	Winnipeg	20:25 - 21:45

EXHIBIT 4	Mileage Between Selected Communities in Manitoba and the Northwest Territories
Destination	**Miles**
Winnipeg - Thompson	409
Winnipeg - Flin Flon	388
Winnipeg - The Pas	326
Winnipeg - Gillam	458
Winnipeg - Churchill	627
Winnipeg - Rankin Inlet	923
Thompson - Flin Flon	171
Thompson - The Pas	207
Thompson - Gillam	127
Thompson - Churchill	249
Thompson - Rankin Inlet	526

EXHIBIT 5	Fares and Passengers Boarded for Selected Routes in Northern Manitoba and Northwest Territories

Winnipeg—Thompson

Fares (return ticket not including taxes)

Full Fare	$576
7 day Advance Fare	$495
14 day Advance Fare	$317
Average Fare *(70% full/15% 7 day/15% 14 day)	$524

Passengers Boarded (one way)

**Canadian North	29000
*Calm Air	12000
Total Boardings	41000

Winnipeg—The Pas

Fares (return ticket not including taxes)

Full Fare	$498
7 day Advance Fare	$428
14 day Advance Fare	$274
Average Fare (60% full/20% 7 day/20% 14 day)	$440

Passengers Boarded (one way)

Canadian North	7500
Calm Air	4500
Total Boardings	12000

Winnipeg—Flin Flon

Fares (return ticket not including taxes)

Full Fare	$538
7 day Advance Fare	$463
14 day Advance Fare	$296
Average Fare (60% full/20% 7 day/20% 14 day)	$475

Passengers Boarded (one way)

Canadian North	5200
Calm Air	7000
Total Boardings	12200

Winnipeg—Gillam

Fares (return ticket not including taxes)

Full Fare	$626
7 day Advance Fare	$538
14 day Advance Fare	$344
Average Fare *(70% full/15% 7 day/15% 14 day)	$571

Passengers Boarded (one way)

**Canadian North	5000
*Calm Air	1500
Total Boardings	6500

Winnipeg - Churchill

Fares (return ticket not including taxes)

Full Fare	$778
7 day Advance Fare	$669
14 day Advance Fare	$428
Average Fare (40% full/30% 7 day/30% 14 day)	$340

Passengers Boarded (one way)

Canadian North	7000
Calm Air	4000
Total Boardings	11000

Winnipeg—Rankin Inlet

Fares (return ticket not including taxes)

Full Fare	$1,262
7 day Advance Fare	$1,010
14 day Advance Fare	$618
Average Fare (40% full/30% 7 day/30% 14 day)	$993

Passengers Boarded (one way)

Canadian North	3500
Calm Air	7000
Total Boardings	10500

*Casewriter estimate
**1993 Statistics Canada

EXHIBIT 6	Aircraft Information				
Aircraft	**Dornier 328-110**	**BA Jetstream J41**	**Beachcraft 1400D**	**SAAB 340B**	**Embrear banditer. "Bandit"**
Payload Passengers	30	29	19	34	15
Payload (Lbs)	8118	7220	6430	7000	4664
Speed (Knots)	345	250	284	272	225
Direct Operating Cost	$4.02/mile	$3.29/mile	$3.76/mile	$4.23/mile	$2.50/mile
Purchase Price Cad $	$12.0	$8.1 MM	$5.4 MM	12.5 MM	—

Note: Yearly fixed costs (include only insurance and financing costs as a percentage of purchase price) were 12.5 percent of the purchase price.

EXHIBIT 7	Advertising and Promotion Costs

1. Free Press
   These prices were based on running an ad on the business page that is 2 columns wide (4.25")
   and 3.5" high.
   Casual/Open Rates:
Sunday	$325.00
Monday to Friday	$625.00 per day
Saturday	$790.00

2. Bus Stop Benches
   $100.00 per bench per month (3-month contract required)
   $125.00 per bench for artwork/setup/installation

3. Hook Billboards
   $650.00 per billboard per month (drops to $600.00 if have 4 billboards)
   $700.00 for artwork/set-up/installation for 2-color billboard ($900.00 total for 4 billboards)

4. Gallop + Gallop
   It did transit-related advertising
   21" x 70"
25 GRPs (31)	$4255.00
50 GRPs (62)	$8165.00

   30" x 139"
25 GRPs (27)	$4945.00
50 GRPs (53)	$9315.00

5. Mediacom
    It did outdoor advertising. Its rates were as follows:

Transit Shelters	4' x 5'	$ 350.00
Billboard	10' x 20'	$ 700.00
Superboard	10' x 44'	$1500.00

    There were the production costs on top of that. For example, the superboard would be about $2250.00 + $11.00 per square foot for anything that juts outside of the 10' x 44' space.

6. Manitoba Business Magazine
    Circulation is 8,000. For one-time advertising its rates were as follows:

1/6 page	$ 515.00 (b&w)	$ 735.00 (color)
1/3 page	$ 990.00 (b&w)	$1415.00 (color)
1/2 page	$1640.00 (b&w)	$2350.00 (color)

7. Weetamah
    It published every two weeks. Its circulation is 9,000 in Manitoba.

1/8 page	$132.00
1/4 page	$264.00
1/3 page	$360.00
1/2 page	$540.00

8. Neechee Culture
    It published every 2 months. Total circulation is 300,000 with 10,000 in Winnipeg and 20,000 in Manitoba. Its rates for black & white ads were as follows:

1/8 page	$250.00
1/4 page	$460.00
1/3 page	$650.00
1/2 page	$900.00

CADBURY'S TimeOut: CHOC AROUND THE CLOCK

Damien McLoughlin[1]
and Benoit Heilbrunn[2]

INTRODUCTION

Cadbury's TimeOut is the most successful product ever developed and launched by Cadbury in Ireland. The development was by the management of Cadbury Ireland, at their plant in Coolock, Dublin. The product's success came from a combination of technological advance, strong domestic and international market orientation and original positioning strategy at the time of launch.

Cadbury started manufacturing in Ireland in the 1930s, at a time when the protectionist policies of the Irish government effectively forbade the importation of chocolate to Ireland. Ireland and the United Kingdom's entry to the EEC in 1973 made them an open market for confectionery. The effect on the industry in Ireland was that several indigenous firms such as Lemons (hard-boiled sweets) and Urnies (chocolates) disappeared from the marketplace. The implication for Cadbury Ireland was the need to reshape its manufacturing so that it was positioned to benefit from economies of scale internationally rather than simply domestically.

Cadbury Ireland As a Partner in Cadbury Schweppes International

Within the Cadbury-Schweppes group, Cadbury Ireland identified its particular strengths and competencies and set out to develop in these areas. The company identified three technologies in which it felt that it had, or could develop global expertise. These three areas were:

1. University College Dublin.
2. Department of Marketing, Graduate School of Business, UCD, Blackrock, Co. Dublin, Ireland.

1. *Extrusion.* This involves putting one form of confectionery inside another: for example, Cadbury's Eclairs wrapped chocolate in caramel; or the Moro bar, which is a centre of chocolate paste with biscuit encased in caramel and covered in chocolate.

2. *Flake chocolate manufacture.* Cadbury's Flake is a light, crumbly, melt-in-the-mouth product positioned in the indulgence section of the confectionery market. The Flake brand is very well established and its advertising is legendary. The brand has been leveraged to include confectionery, catering and ice-cream usage. However, the Flake recipe and process provide unique product properties, which were the key for future development.

3. *Wafer making and baking.* Wafer is an important part of a number of strong-selling products in Ireland, in particular the 'pink Snack brand'. Cadbury Ireland is the only Cadbury-Schweppes affiliate in the northern hemisphere to manufacture the wafer product.

Building On Core Competencies at Cadbury Ireland

Since the mid 1970s Cadbury Ireland had developed centres of excellence around these core competencies. The strong product development process in Cadbury Ireland had produced products such as Cadbury's Chomp, Moro, TimeOut and Twirl. Twirl is a two-finger casual chocolate snack based on flake technology. These developments have led to a doubling of Cadbury Ireland's throughput and allowed it to develop its brand successfully on both the domestic and international markets.

The Perspective of Cadbury Ireland On the Marketplace

Cadbury sees itself as a 'range house'. This describes a company which provides the consumer with a complete range of options in every segment of the market. In addition, all Cadbury products bear the distinctive Cadbury logo. The core product of the Cadbury group is Dairy Milk chocolate, which is used in its products and which is also marketed under the Dairy Milk brand name. This chocolate, which uses fresh Irish milk, has been the basis of success in a great number of segments. Cadbury defines segments on the basis of how customers buy rather than on how a product is made. For example, they identify products as serving impulse markets, take-home markets or gift usage. This has allowed Cadbury Ireland management to identify a significant consumption pattern whereby the take-home segment is increasing its share of the confectionery market. This trend is driven by supermarket purchases of chocolate. In addition, they had noticed a certain overlap in the marketplace where brands which were traditionally seen as bars — for example, Twix and KitKat — were extending their franchise into the biscuit market. The main snack brands in Ireland (see Exhibit 10.1) are as follows:

- KitKat. KitKat was first sold in Ireland in 1937. It has become one of the most popular brands on the market with in the region of 1£11m.[3] sales in 1992. KitKat had initiated the move into the biscuit market with the memorable advert debating '…it's a biscuit…it's a bar'. This ad showed the product being used in different ways and suggested that it had

---

3. 1 ecu = US$1.26 = 1£0.81 (Irish Punt) = 81p.

multiple uses. Nestlé-Rowntree, the owners of the brand, maintained this position by heavy advertising and maintaining the price of the product at a below market par level. Usually 2 to 4p below its main competitors, KitKat is also available in bar and snack size formats.

- Twix. Owned by the Mars corporation, Twix was launched in Ireland in 1968. The effort was made to develop a position for the product in the snack market with the advertising slogan 'Whenever there is a snack gap, Twix fits'. Its packaging format, in a flow wrapper, however, also allowed it to fit in to the bar/impulse market segment. The success of Twix has been attributed to its good value-for-money position and the heavy advertising support that it has traditionally received. Total brand sales in 1992 were estimated to be in the region of 1£6-7m. Twix was among the first products to be sold in the snack and fun-size formats.

EXHIBIT 10.1	The Main Snack Brands in Ireland, 1992		
	Manufacturer	**Launched**	**Sales (1£m.)**
KitKat	Nestlé-Rowntree	1937	11.0
Twix	Mars	1968	6.5
Jacobs Club Milk	Jacobs	1900s	5.0
Cadbury's Snack	Cadbury	1960s	11.0

- Jacob's Club Milk. The oldest brand on the market, Jacob's Club Milk has been sold in Ireland since the 1900s. It is sold singly and in family six-pack formats. The Club Milk acts as a flagship for a range of different flavoured, chocolate-covered Club biscuits. For example, the Club bar is available in Club Orange and Club Mint formats. The position of Club Milk in the snack market is firmly achieved with the advertising message 'If you're going to have a cuppa have a Club'.

- Cadbury's Snack. Since its launch in the 1960s, the Cadbury's Snack brand has grown to lead the chocolate snack market. This domination is achieved through grocery sales but also includes the important catering market. The Snack comes in three formats, differentiated by the colour of the packaging. The 'yellow' snack comprises a chocolate-covered shortcake biscuit. The 'purple' snack is a sandwich-filled biscuit heavily covered with thick milk chocolate. The third option is the 'pink' snack, which comprises three fingers of chocolate-covered wafer. Cadbury's Snack is sold in a variety of formats incorporating single bar, multipacks and treat size. Its combined sales from grocery, newsagent and catering outlets were in excess of 1£11m. in 1992.

The Snack Market

The snack is a particularly prominent product market in Great Britain and Ireland. It is essentially a lifestyle market linked to a destructured approach to food. Snack products are most successful in those countries in which eating habits are not centred around two or three main meals. In these countries the consumption of food may be scattered around various occasions during the day. Thus the 11 a.m. and 4 p.m. snack breaks are usual practice in Irish and English lifestyles. These breaks generally consist of a cup of tea/coffee together with fruit, a chocolate bar or a scone. Internationally, this snack habit is linked to the grazing phenomenon, which is representative of the slow but steady change in cultural habits concerning eating (destruction of family meals and less time devoted to meals) and accounts for the growth of the snack market in other European countries. That the Irish are accomplished 'snackers' is evidenced by their large confectionery market with annual sales in 1992 of over 1£240m. (see Exhibit 10.2).

EXHIBIT 10.2	The Confectionery Market in Ireland				
	1988	1989	1990	1991	1992
Estimated market value at RSP (1£m.)	210	216	228	245	242
Annual growth rate (%)	—	3.0	5.0	3.0	2.9

Source: Nestlé-Rowntree

Break Time In Ireland

Ireland is also a great tea-drinking nation. A survey carried out by Nielsen in 1993 in Ireland showed that twenty of the top 100 grocery brands are liquid consumables. However, leading tea brands in Ireland are positioned on value for money rather than taste. This means that tea might be viewed as a depersonalized drink. Therefore there is considerable need for a beverage complement with strong personality in order to personalize break times.

In trying to meet this need Cadbury were faced with what was a mature marketplace. Irish consumption of confectionery is the highest in Europe (see Exhibit 10.3). Chocolate consumption alone is 8.3 kilos per annum per capita. This figure is matched only by their British neighbours.

The Concept of TimeOut

Based on these trends in the marketplace and Cadbury's core technological competencies, the management of Cadbury Ireland saw the opportunity to bring confectionery values to the biscuit market and biscuit values to the confectionery market. In this sense TimeOut set out specifically to target the bridge-brand position and satisfy all uses from mainstream confectionery luxury to straight beverage accompaniment, but with values firmly rooted in the break market.

It also had to compete with existing competitors in this market, particularly KitKat and Twix, both brands which had also targeted the bridge-brand position for the future. TimeOut therefore 'institutionalized' the coexistence of three elements: the need for a break during the day, tea or coffee as a liquid consumable, and the need for a snack to accompany that drink. This can be paraphrased as 'wherever you are, whatever you are doing, when it's that time (i.e. your time for a break) it's TimeOut time'.

EXHIBIT 10.3		EU Consumption of Confectionery (kg per capita)									
	Ireland	UK	Greece	Belgium	Denmark	West Germany	France	Nether-lands	Italy	Spain	Portugal	EU average
Chocolate	8.3	8.3	2.4	7.0	7.2	5.9	5.2	6.0	1.3	2.3	0.5	4.8
Biscuits	17.9	13.0	17.9	5.2	5.5	3.1	6.5	2.8	5.9	5.2	4.6	6.6
Ice cream	8.0	7.1	5.3	9.8	9.1	7.8	4.7	4.5	6.1	3.8	1.8	6.0
Total	34.2	28.4	25.6	22.0	21.8	16.8	16.4	13.3	13.3	11.3	6.9	17.1

Source: In *Irish Consumer Market Handbook: A guidebook for marketing managers,* ed. M. V. Lambkin (Dublin: Marketing Society of Ireland, 1993), adapted from *European Marketing Data and Statistics,* 27th ed. (London: Euromonitor, 1992).

The Positioning Mix for the Launch of TimeOut

Product

TimeOut stems from a technological advance at Cadbury Ireland which allowed them to layer flake on to wafer. The competitive advantage of this product lies in the unique blend of flake sandwiched between two wafers and covered in dairy milk chocolate. In product terms, TimeOut bridges both the snack and bar markets as the Flake ingredient was sufficiently biscuity to be a suitable accompaniment to a beverage break. On the one hand its biscuit constituency made it an ideal snack, while its Flake content made it a suitable bar of chocolate in its own right.

The Branding Ingredients: Brand Name, Logo and Identity Colours

Many names were proposed for the new product including 'Switch' and 'Ultra'. However, it was discovered that using a name indicating the timing and situation in which the bar should be consumed greatly enhanced the consumer's understanding of what the product was designed for. The TimeOut name was proposed and accepted as it more clearly communicated the desired position as *the snack* accompaniment. These brand-name objectives were supported by the use of a clock (suggesting that any time is suitable for TimeOut) and a mug (which reinforced the beverage break accompaniment role).

The new brand needed a strong visual identity system to reinforce the other positioning elements. Hence the use of bold primary colours on the packaging to attract attention and create competitive distinction. The two main colours used were blue, considered the main identity colour, and red, which is used to write the brand name. The brand name is surrounded by yellow: this blue/red/yellow association is the colour scheme most easily associated with light biscuity bars. Blue also has a symbolic connotation and is considered as a peaceful and resting colour. The choice of colour is interesting because the market is dominated by darker brand colours such as black/brown (Mars) and gold (Twix).

Pricing

Consumer knowledge of price in the snack market, given its habitual nature, is high. However, the standard-size chocolate bars are only slightly differentiated in terms of price. Given the power of retailers, the producer often has little discretion in the determination of price. TimeOut was launched at a price of 28p, while a standard bar was priced at 30p.

Packaging Configuration

Packaging was particularly important in positioning TimeOut as a bridge brand. Most brands establish themselves in standard format initially and then expand to different formats. TimeOut, however, was required to meet the needs of a number of groups and so came in a variety of formats from the start:

- Standard. The standard product to be sold in newsagents, workplace restaurants and coffee shops. The format is two full-size fingers in a flow wrapper. In newsagents or supermarkets TimeOut is placed with other Cadbury brands.
- 5-pack. The five-pack format was five TimeOut fingers in a convenience pack to allow the product to be bought in bulk from supermarkets. It is positioned with the multipacks for other confectionery products.
- Breakpack. The breakpack consisted of six shorter twin-finger packs individually wrapped. This is also sold in supermarkets and is intended for the home snack market. In supermarkets the breakpack would be put on shelf space with the biscuit range.
- Treat-size. The treat-size format is intended to meet the demands of the children's treat/party market. The treat-size format was 14 full-size individually wrapped TimeOut fingers. These are mainly distributed through supermarkets. The shelf position for the treat size is with the treat and fun-size formats of other confectionery products.

Advertising and Promotion

At is initial launch in early 1992 TimeOut was supported by a complete range of advertising and promotion. Heavy TV and radio advertising emphasized the 'TimeOut at any time' theme. Promotions included balloon releases at several centres around the country, a variety of street activities involving a national radio station and using branded characters, and participation at the annual St. Patrick's Day parade in Dublin. Free samples were generously distributed at street activities and during in-store promotions. TimeOut has also made effective and large-scale use of poster advertising.

TimeOut used both family brand promotions and brand alliance promotions in its initial positioning. An example of the family brand promotions was one with Lyons tea, the largest selling brand of tea in Ireland. The promotion gave customers a free bar of TimeOut with every standard box of tea. This achieved two goals. First, given the market share of Lyons, it facilitated trial of the product. Secondly, it was an opportunity to nail down the position of TimeOut as a beverage accompaniment. The overall promotional message was one of a new, friendly, modern, fun and young, beverage-break accompaniment that was suitable for use at any time.

The Success of TimeOut

Six to eight months after its launch a national trade magazine completed a brand evaluation of TimeOut (*Checkout,* July/August 1993). Primary research completed by an independent research company highlighted some extraordinary results.

User Profile

The user profile of the brand demonstrated a widespread acceptance. The vast majority of adults and all children had used the brand at some stage since its introduction (see Exhibit 10.4). Women, a prime market for chocolate consumption, represented over 60 per cent of TimeOut consumers. Users were drawn from all areas of Ireland but were particularly strong in urban areas. This user profile was assisted by a high conversion ratio for both adults and children (see Exhibit 10.5).

Attitudes Towards the Brand

As might be expected given the high levels of trial achieved for the brand, consumer attitudes towards the brand were very positive (see Exhibit 10.6). This is particularly evidenced by the positive appeal which the brand had for both adults and children. Among the target group of 11–25 year olds there was virtually no criticism of the brand. This sort of consumer support should allow TimeOut to build on its initial success even after its large-scale media support is reduced.

EXHIBIT 10.4 Brand Acceptance Among Adults and Children (%)	Adults (15 years +)	Children (11–14 years)
Aware	86	100
Ever used	68	97
Used once/twice	23	13
Occasional user	22	41
Regular user	14	43

Source: Lansdowne Market Research

EXHIBIT 10.5 Cadbury's TimeOut Conversion Ratio (%)	Adults (15 years +)	Children (11–14 years)
Awareness to trial	69	97
Trial to repeat user	61	87
Won over consumers	66	86
Lost consumers	7	1

Source: Lansdowne Market Research.

EXHIBIT 10.6	Cadbury's TimeOut Brand Appeal (%)	
	Adults (15 years +)	**Children (11–14 years)**
Positive	66	86
Neutral	27	14
Negative	7	1

Questions

1. What criteria did Cadbury Ireland use in developing TimeOut? What role did they play in the positioning strategy of TimeOut?

2. TimeOut has adopted what it describes as a 'bridge-brand' position. What are the risks of the 'bridge-brand' position? Which marketing mix variables were most important in positioning TimeOut?

3. How did the positioning and marketing strategies of its main competitors influence TimeOut's positioning?

4. Discuss the promotional strategy used to launch TimeOut. What are the cultural factors that account for the success of TimeOut? Could TimeOut be successful in other European countries?

WEST OAKS SHOPPING CENTRE

Ivey

WEST OAKS SHOPPING CENTRE

In mid-1997, Kathy Odegaard, centre manager for West Oaks Shopping Centre, was considering a proposal put to her by Ian Bramwell, a doctoral candidate from the local university. Ian summed up his ideas with:

> So, as I've said, what I'd like to do, Ms. Odegaard, is to make you the subject of my doctoral dissertation. I'm interested in retail research and would like to study how you are positioned in the Vanloops marketplace. I propose to do a consumer study that would tell us how you are regarded by citizens in Vanloops, how often they buy from your centre as opposed to the other centres, what they like and dislike about you, and so on. I'm willing to do all the work, but I'd need your permission and cooperation, and about $25,000 for the direct-out-of-pocket costs

for the research. I'm currently thinking about a mail survey and a two-week shopping diary, tracking where people shop and how much they spend.

Kathy was intrigued, but Ian's request for $25,000 for expenses meant that she needed to be sure that the research was relevant to her needs and properly done. West Oaks hadn't done any research to speak of for over eight years. She chose her words carefully:

Ian, I'm willing to say we will go ahead with you on the condition that, together, we develop a complete research design that meets my needs for managing the centre. You can figure out for yourself whether that will meet your needs for your thesis. I'll give it some thought. Let's find a time when we can get together again in about a week's time.

After Ian left, Kathy began to organize her thoughts about market research for the centre.

GENERAL DESCRIPTION OF VANLOOPS

Metropolitan Vanloops was a major city in British Columbia. With a population of 258,700 as of June 1996, Vanloops had experienced a growth in population of just over seven per cent since 1991. Personal income was 11 per cent above the Canadian national average, representing about $20,300 per capita. There were 105,445 private households in Vanloops and 70,210 families. About 80 per cent of the population had English as their mother tongue. Retail sales per capita were $8,800 in 1996. There was one daily newspaper, *The Times*, and at least nine area community newspapers. Residents of metropolitan Vanloops could receive approximately 20 radio stations and 24 television stations.

SHOPPING CENTRES IN VANLOOPS

There were 15 shopping centres in the West Oaks market area. Kathy summarized some key information about the six centres she considered her major competitors as well as information about her own centre, as shown in Exhibit 1. Kathy was concerned that Vanloops was becoming overmalled. She was particularly concerned about rumored expansion plans for two of her competitors. Kathy wondered if her advertising theme "Your First Place For Fashion" was competitively powerful. She also wondered if her customers were unhappy about any aspect of the mall, such as the store assortment, parking, washrooms, baby strollers, etc. Kathy particularly wondered if her major competitors had some weak spots she could exploit in her own marketing campaigns.

THE RESEARCH IDEA

Ian had suggested a questionnaire be sent to residents of Vanloops, along with a "shopping diary" asking them to keep records of where they shopped and what they bought for two weeks. Kathy wondered if anybody would respond. And how many responses would be enough to have any confidence in the results? Should she offer some kind of incentive to increase the response rate? It would certainly be less expensive to hand out questionnaires in her own mall, but would that be wise? And how would she know whether a question was well-worded? She realized she had lots of questions.

Kathy felt West Oaks should work with Ian rather than let him work with her competition. She knew he had approached her first because his mother was a regular shopper at West Oaks. However, she knew her owner, Isaac Property Corporation, would insist that she proceed only if the research was very professionally handled. She wondered where she should begin.

EXHIBIT 1	Selected Vanloops Shopping Centres

West Oaks Centre

Quadrant	N
Year Opened:	1963 (renovated 1984)
Type:	Regional, enclosed, one level
Stores:	105
Gross leasable area:	375,000 sq. ft.
Parking:	1,800
Anchors:	The Bay 169,000; Future Shop 11,500

Hidden Valley Shopping Centre

Quadrant:	N
Year Opened:	1963 (renovation 1990)
Type:	Regional, enclosed, one level
Stores:	14
Gross leasable area:	206,431 sq. ft.
Anchors:	Wal-Mart 125,077; Extra Foods 24,316; Shoppers Drug Mart 5,079

Sandwich Plaza

Quadrant:	N
Year Opened:	1986
Type:	Neighborhood, open, one level
Stores:	22
Gross leasable area:	116,000 sq. ft.
Anchors:	Save-on-Foods 75,000

University Hill Shopping Centre

Quadrant:	Central
Year Opened:	1987
Type:	Neighborhood, enclosed, three levels
Stores:	85
Gross leasable area:	200,000 sq. ft.
Anchors:	Safeway 38,000; Kmart 84,000; Royal Bank 5,500

Trillium Mall

Quadrant:	W
Year Opened:	1982 (renovation 1990)
Type:	Regional, enclosed, two levels
Stores:	75
Gross leasable area:	331,584 sq. ft.
Anchors:	Eaton's 120,000; Zellers 65,000; Safeway 35,000

Coldwater Mall

Quadrant:	E
Year Opened:	1984
Type:	Community, enclosed, one level
Stores:	50
Gross leasable area:	210,000 sq. ft.
Anchors:	Kmart 75,000; Save-on-Foods 40,000

Downstream Shopping Centre

Quadrant:	S
Year Opened:	1962 (renovation 1985, 1991)
Type:	Regional, enclosed, one level
Stores:	125
Gross leasable area:	398,536 sq. ft.
Anchors:	Sears 118,535; Zellers 75,090; The Market 40,000

STREBER INC. DEALER OUTLET SURVEY (A)

8

IVEY

In the last week of January 1991, Al Mikal, the president of Streber Inc., had to decide how to inform his key people about the results of a recent dealer survey relating to Streber's quality of service to its independent dealers. As well, he was wondering about the best way to initiate and implement a change program to make Streber more competitive in its service offerings.

He had just received what he considered to be the devastating results of the Dealer Outlet Survey which had investigated retailer assessments of the various customer-related services rendered by Streber Inc. and the other 19 firms which had sponsored the study. While the trade members generally thought well of Streber's salesforce, they were most unhappy with just about every other aspect of their interaction with Streber Inc. From order entry to delivery and invoicing, Streber was consistently rated in the bottom quartile.

THE COMPANY

Background

Streber Inc. was founded by David Mikal in the late 1930s. In 1960, Al and Edward Mikal, David Mikal's sons, who had been active in the business all their lives, took control of the company. Sales in 1990 amounted to $17,000,000, and for the previous decade they had been growing at an annual rate of six to seven per cent. Profits after taxes, executive salaries, and dividends were $400,000 in 1990 on a book equity of $4,000,000.

The company had 100 employees located at the 100,000 square foot modern plant in MacDonald, Ontario (population 4,000, 20 kilometers southwest of Owen Sound, Ontario) where the Mikal family resided. There were eight employees in the marketing office in Mississauga, Ontario (a Toronto suburb). Exhibit 1 shows Streber's organization chart.

Product Line

Streber's product line was fairly broad. Total company sales were divided: 25 per cent from vitamin products (half of these were multi-vitamins); 25 per cent from hair treatment products; and 50 per cent from "over the counter" (OTC), medically-oriented products such as laxatives, cough medicines, and pain reducers. Market share position for Streber brands in their respective categories tended to be number three or lower. Regional sales volumes tended to follow population levels, except that Streber historically had relatively low sales in the province of Quebec. With the exception of the hair treatment product line, which was sold under a separate brand name, each product was labeled to some degree as a Streber product. The size and prominence of the company name, however, varied from one product to another.

Streber faced branded competition from both major international pharmaceutical corporations and smaller national firms. The vitamin market was typical of the competition faced by most Streber products. It included global companies such as Lederle (Centrum), Miles (One-A-Day), Johnson and Johnson (Sesame Street), and Ayerst (Paramettes), all of which had significant financial and human resources. They tended to hold significant market shares in the categories in which they competed. Jamieson and Webber were Canadian-based competitors with some market strengths in some product categories. In addition, there were companies in major centres such as Toronto that were exclusively dedicated to manufacturing private label brands for retail drug chains, voluntary chains and department stores, and other chains with pharmacy departments.

The sale of vitamin products had grown dramatically in Canada over the previous two decades. Multi-vitamins had become a year-round product line as many consumers moved to daily consumption; however, other lines, such as vitamin C, were still primarily consumed in the winter. Over the past decade, the industry sales growth in vitamins had been largely captured by retail drug chain house brands. Shoppers Drug Mart's controlled label, Life, was accepted by many in the industry as the largest selling and most highly advertised vitamin brand in Canada. Streber, supported by the efforts of its 30-person sales team composed of 27 sales representatives and three district managers had competed successfully in the vitamin category by offering a broad product line, with particular strength in distribution in independent and smaller regional chain outlets.

Distribution

The distribution of Streber vitamin products in the few major drug chains, such as Shoppers Drug Mart, which had strong house brand coverage, was limited to: (a) smaller volume specialized vitamin categories where the chain had no product entry in the category; (b) smaller but growing volume categories where the chain had not yet chosen to develop a house brand, and; (c) one fairly high volume product category where the Streber brand name held a reasonably strong brand franchise. Shoppers was a significant force in the industry with 650 franchised outlets throughout Canada. Industry estimates were that in some product categories it held more than 40 per cent of the total Canadian retail druggists' sales volume.

The distribution of Streber's non-vitamin lines was even more closely tied to the independent and smaller regional chain outlets. Recently, the emergence of some high volume discount challengers, such as Hy and Zel's in the Ontario market, had helped Streber's volume. Because these outlets did not have significant sales of their own house brands, they tended to feature Streber's products at low prices in their promotional materials.

Seasonality was a factor for many of Streber's product lines, and booking orders in advance on "deals" was standard industry practice. Summer products typically were booked by the sales team in the first quarter of the calendar year for delivery in April or May, depending on the climate of the region. Billing was for payment in September, with full-return privileges on any remaining inventory as of the billing date. Everyone in the industry complained about the problems associated with this early booking and late paying practice that all too often resulted in overloaded dealer outlets, distorted sales figures, and expensive returns. However, no one did anything to change the situation.

Streber's products went directly from the plant in MacDonald, Ontario, to retail outlets. A minor exception was sales to department stores and to the other chains which operated drug departments where delivery was made to their central warehouse for redistribution to individual stores.

Sales

Most orders were generated by the sales force on their calls, and then mailed, faxed or phoned to the order desk at the plant. A small but increasing number of orders was telephoned directly by druggists to the order desk, which offered a toll-free telephone number to dealers located in the populated areas of Ontario and Quebec. One person handled the order desk, which was open from 8:30 a.m. to 4:30 p.m. EST, Monday through Friday. Relief was provided by one of the clerical staff to cover coffee breaks, lunches, holidays, and absences. The order desk relief person was fluent in both English and French. The full-time person spoke English only. Both order desk personnel reported to the plant office manager in MacDonald.

The sales force was compensated on an 80 per cent salary and 20 per cent bonus basis, with the bonus tied to both volume sales achievement and to other performance factors such as promptness, completeness and pertinence of weekly sales reports, new product introduction accomplishments and special projects, etc. Sales personnel turnover of five per cent per year was below industry average. As a result, the Streber sales force was composed of many "veterans" who had covered the same territory and accounts for many years. The sales force had been increased by five people over the previous three years. Sales force allocation across the country tended to follow provincial sales levels. As of December 1990, there were five salespeople based in Quebec, eleven in Ontario, three in the Maritime Provinces, and eight in the West.

DEALER OUTLET SURVEY

The Dealer Outlet Survey had been designed by a major research house to help manufacturers of pharmaceuticals and health and beauty products improve their understanding of dealer outlet needs and expectations. The survey considered the performance of major manufacturers on a number of the elements considered to be of key importance to independent druggists: sales representative performance, order entry, delivery, terms-of-sale and billing/accounting/credit.

The survey consisted of two phases. In the first phase, mail questionnaires were sent to store owners/managers of independent drug outlets. The second phase involved in-depth personal interviews with a selection of owners/managers who had completed the survey questionnaire. There were 500 completed questionnaires supported by 20 personal interviews with druggists.

The survey was paid for by Streber and 19 other firms in the health and beauty aids industry. Although similar studies had apparently been done for the industry previously, this was the first time Streber had been involved. Streber was one of the smallest firms involved in the survey. The company's participation in this particular study was part of a continuing process of information generation by the sales and marketing groups at Streber. In Mikal's opinion, his company, for far too long, had relied almost solely upon the "G.O.B." (Good Old Boy) system of relying upon sales force inputs about market and trade realities based upon the sales force interactions with the trade. He had brought in people such as Cathy Howell and Don Shaw, who had experience in consumer package goods sales and marketing, with the expectation that they would use the data from consumer reports and surveys such as this to introduce a more sophisticated, analytical approach to Streber's marketing decision making.

COMMUNICATING SURVEY RESULTS

The results of the study, (see Exhibits 2, 3, and 4) in Mikal's view, were devastating for Streber. Obviously the trade with whom Streber dealt were most unhappy with the way in which they were being treated. The degree of unhappiness differed somewhat according to province or size of outlets served by Streber, but Mikal did not consider these differences important. There was no significant difference between Streber's being in the third versus the fourth quartile, as neither position was acceptable.

Mikal knew that Howell, the marketing manager, and Shaw, the sales manager, were eagerly awaiting the results, as Streber's participation in the study had been a direct result of their suggestion. The other key people in the organization had been advised at one of the quarterly managers' meetings that the study was to be undertaken, but since they had not asked about its arrival in spite of several delays, he did not expect any real pressure from them for disclosure.

Mikal realized, however, that since the health and beauty aid industry was Toronto-based, he should expect that bits and pieces of the study results would be "on the street" soon. More important, he realized that a good buyer-seller relationship was key to Streber's success in the business. Due to low consumer brand loyalty for Streber's products in general, trade-push had been Streber's primary strategic choice.

Because he had scheduled a meeting with both Howell and Shaw that week on other matters, the opportunity existed to go over the report with them. The regularly scheduled quarterly managers' meeting, for which he had yet to develop an agenda, was due in two weeks time. Also, the program for the annual sales meeting in two months was not yet finalized. Since all the sales and marketing teams, and all department heads and other key people in the company would be attending, this annual meeting presented a unique opportunity for communicating with virtually all areas of the company.

Because Al Mikal was in contact with his brother, Edward, vice president of manufacturing, almost daily, advising him presented no scheduling problem. That Edward had not enquired about the survey after it was undertaken was not surprising, as he tended to focus almost exclusively on manufacturing issues.

EXHIBIT 1   Organization

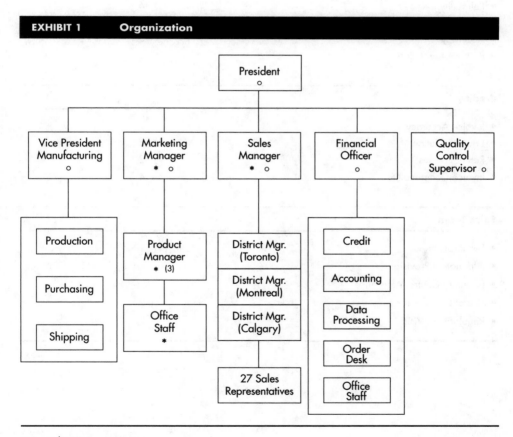

* Located in Mississauga
o Members of The Management Committee

EXHIBIT 2	Survey Results—National Ranking
Selected Aspects of Performance	**Streber Quartile Ranking**

Order Desk

• Accessibility	3
• Information Provided	4
• Attitude of Personnel	4
• Product Knowledge of Personnel	4

Delivery

• Back Order Frequency	3
• Reliability	4
• Promptness	4
• Accuracy	3
• Problem Resolution	3

Credit

• Invoice Accuracy	3
• Error Resolution	3
• Return Policies	2
• Invoice Compatibility	4

Sales Team

• Responsiveness	1
• Information Provision	2
• Inventory Control Assistance	1
• Use of Dealer's Time	2
• Regularity of Visits	2

EXHIBIT 3	Survey Results—Regional Ranking Example

Selected Aspects of Performance	Streber Quartile Ranking						
	Mar	Qu	On	M	S	Al	BC
Order Desk							
• Accessibility	4	4	3	4	4	3	3
• Information Provided	4	3	3	3	4	4	3
• Attitude of Personnel	4	4	4	4	4	3	3
• Product Knowledge of Personnel	3	4	4	4	4	3	3

Legend

Mar	Maritime	S	Saskatchewan
Qu	Quebec	A	Alberta
On	Ontario	BC	British Columbia
M	Manitoba		

EXHIBIT 4	Survey Results—Ranking by Outlet Size

Selected Aspects of Performance	Streber Quartile Ranking		
		Outlet Size	
	Small	Medium	Large
Order Desk			
• Accessibility	3	4	4
• Information Provided	3	4	4
• Attitude of Personnel	3	4	4
• Product Knowledge of Personnel	3	4	4

DIESEL JEANS & WORKWEAR:

'We're all different, but aren't we all different in the same way?'[1]

Malin Nilsson,
Anki Sjöström,
Anneli Zell,
and Thomas Helgesson[2]

During the oil-crisis in 1978, the idea of a trademark called Diesel came to Renzo Rosso, the son of an Italian farmer. To him Diesel represented something that everybody needs and always will need. He kept this in mind until 1985, when the real Diesel story began. In that year he decided to produce and sell clothes that he himself liked to wear; clothes that represented his lifestyle. His wild and masculine 'Renzo Rosso style' is what Diesel jeans and Workwear is all about. It is a way of living…

Get Your Blue Jeans On

Blue jeans are the most successful clothes ever invented and the world's largest clothing companies depend on them. Why has this 'all American' workwear become the global uniform? Sociologist John Fiske tries to explain. He once asked a class to write down what jeans meant to each of them. He got back a set of staggeringly uniform results. Jeans were American, informal, classless, unisex and appropriate in town or country. Wearing them was a sign of freedom from constraints on behaviour and of class membership. *Free* was the word most commonly used, usually expressing 'freedom to be oneself'. By wearing jeans Fiske's class were expressing their 'freedom to be themselves', yet 118 out of 125 students were 'being themselves' by wearing the same clothes, jeans. With everyone wearing the same clothes, people who are really free go one step further to express themselves. Rockers wore greasy ones, mods smart ones, hippies old ones, skinheads new ones, punks damaged ones, indies torn ones and grunge shabby ones—but all wore jeans.

---

1. The quotation is copy from a 1970s Levi ad.
2. Halmstad University, Sweden.

Fashion Bubbles Up

Jeans are no longer as uniform, or cheap, as they used to be. The generic jeans, foundation of the Levi Strauss and Wrangler empires, mean classless, country, communal, unisex, work, traditional, unchanging and American. But not so designer jeans. These reached their zenith when Pakistan-born Shami Ahmed exhibited his Manchester-made, diamond-studded, Joe Bloggs jeans costing £150,000[3] a pair. In contrast to generic jeans, designer jeans mean up-market, city, socially distinctive, (usually) feminine leisure, contemporary, transient and not American. So transient and non-American are Joe Bloggs jeans that the range changes twelve times a year and West Indian cricketer, Brian Lara, promotes their 375 and 501 range. The ranges are named after Lara's record breaking batting scores although Levi are not happy about the Joe Bloggs 501 name.

Jeans are not only high fashion but the foundation for many new fashions. Jeans are the uniform of the street culture, and leading designers, such as Versace, Westwood, Gaultier and Lagerfield, concede that there is now a very strong 'bubble up' effect where the streets lead fashion. Top jeans companies 'bubble up' in the same way as street fashions do. Shami Ahmed and Renzo Rosso are typical of the clothing entrepreneurs who are leading the way in Europe's dynamic and varied fashion market, and foremost among these businesses is Rosso's Diesel Jeans & Workwear, a European firm that aims to overtake Levi's and become the world's number-one jeans company.

Diesel's Concept

To work for Rosso, you have to understand the Diesel concept. You have to love Diesel and devote your life to the company. This company spirit imbues the whole organization and is presumably the reason for Diesel's success. For example, Diesel is probably the only company where all employees, even the management team, wear Diesel clothes.

Rosso has managed to create a multinational concern out of Diesel. The turnover is approximately L8,000,000 million* and rising. The profit margin of between 10 and 15 per cent is almost all reinvested in the company. This makes Diesel very strong financially. Today Diesel is number two in Europe after the American jeans-giant Levi's. Their goal is to become number one.

Diesel is today represented in sixty-nine countries worldwide. Of Diesel's 3,000 employees 150 work at their headquarters at Moldava, Italy. Small family-owned companies in Northern Italy carry out about 70 per cent of production, and the rest is spread around low-cost countries like Hong Kong, Thailand and Korea.

The Diesel collection contains jeans, jackets, sweaters, shoes, underwear and belts for both men and women. These account for 60 per cent of Diesel's products. The remainder includes sportswear, kidswear and perfume for men. Diesel's products are sold through hand-picked agents, licensees and subsidiaries. Franchising is not popular as there is a risk of losing control of the company profile. Education and training of the international network is intensive. The resellers have a lot to live up to. They have to understand the Diesel concept and sell clothes that go well with Diesel.

Diesel has only two shops of its own, one in Berlin and the other in Stockholm. New stores in Paris, Rome and New York will open soon. There were strategic reasons for opening the

---

3. 1 ecu = US$1.26 = UK£0.83 = L2,066 (Italian lire).

first two flagship stores in Stockholm and Berlin. Germany is Diesel's largest market: 25 per cent of production is sold there. Sweden is seen as receptive to new fashions and useful for test-marketing. Also, Diesel's vice-president and head of international marketing, Johan Lindeberg, is Swedish. Together with local advertising agency Paradiset, he directs all Diesel's marketing activities from his Swedish headquarters.

Diesel's Advertising

Lindeberg and Paradiset claim that much of their marketing success derives from their lack of respect for marketing strategies and their trend-setting advertising. Adverts are sent by courier-post from 'Paradiset' to distributors in other countries who decide the local marketing arrangements themselves. Local distributors spend 5 per cent of their turnover on national marketing, while Diesel spend 7 percent of their total turnover on internationals such as MTV and Sky Sport.

'Paradiset' has two ideas in mind when creating an advert. The ad should be conspicuous and also contain an ironic message. Diesel's advertising is targeted at modern intelligent people. Diesel often makes fun of current myths, as, for example, in their 'How to. . .' campaign. In this campaign, one advert showed the cranium of a girl sucking on a cigarette. The text read, 'How to smoke 145 a day' and 'Man, who needs two lungs anyway'? This message caused much controversy in the United States, where Diesel were criticized for encouraging young people to smoke.

Rosso has his own way of running a company. He follows his own path, ignoring conventional marketing approaches—and it certainly works! Diesel has great growth potential. Rosso believes that, in the long run, a good organization structure is much more important than good advertising. According to Rosso, a strong company is one 'with strong collaborators'. This requires work that employees enjoy, and above all, work that they find interesting. 'When you trust your own and your collaborators' intuitions, feelings and judgements, and not only text-book theories,' says Rosso, 'then you have reached the Diesel feeling.' Since Rosso owns 100 per cent of Diesel he has his hands free to do whatever he wants. To buy other companies or to be listed on the stock exchange is not 'the Renzo Rosso style' and neither would he leave Moldava. The company's vision is expressed in their slogan, you need Diesel 'for successful living'.

Sources: John Fiske, Understanding Popular Culture (Routledge: London, 1990); Hunter Davies, 'Not any old Joe Bloggs', Independent (15 November 1994), 23; and Stephanie Theobald, 'European street style', The European-élan (11–17 November, 1994), 13–16.

Questions

1. Since jeans are street-led fashions, do jeans companies have to follow, not create, the demand for their products? Are sociologists correct in their perception of the cultural significance of jeans or are they merely inexpensive, practical clothes? How and why have European jeans producers been able to edge into the traditionally American jeans market?

2. How does the advertising for *generic and designer jeans* differ? Can one brand and advertising campaign straddle both markets? Explain Joe Bloggs' choice of Lara and the

£150,000 jeans as a way of promoting the brand. Are twelve ranges a year really necessary?

3. What explains Rosso's choice of Sweden, rather than Italy, as the base for his international marketing activity? Why choose an agency and location outside the London and New York heartlands of modern global advertising? Can 'the Renzo Rosso style' be separated from the brand identity and the advertising used? Are such organizational issues separate from the marketing of the products? How well does 'the Renzo Rosso style' fit the needs of the jeans market and why?

4. What is the controversial style of Diesel's advertising trying to achieve? Do you think it is effective? Ethical? Appropriate for all markets? How does the centralized nature of Diesel's advertising fit the entrepreneurial style of the company? How can the advertising be linked in with the rest of the marketing mix in the many markets and distributors that Diesel serves?